IMAGES OF WAR SPECIAL

THE PANTHER TANK

Disabled Panther tank captured at San Giovanni, Italy, 1944.

IMAGES OF WAR SPECIAL

THE PANTHER TANK
HITLER'S T-34 KILLER

RARE PHOTOGRAPHS FROM WARTIME ARCHIVES

Anthony Tucker-Jones

Illustrated by
David Lee Hemingway

Pen & Sword
MILITARY

First published in Great Britain in 2016 by
PEN & SWORD MILITARY
an imprint of
Pen & Sword Books Ltd,
47 Church Street,
Barnsley,
South Yorkshire
S70 2AS

A CIP record for this book is available from the British Library.

ISBN 978 1 47383 360 9

Typeset by CHIC GRAPHICS

Printed and bound by Gutenberg Press, Malta

Pen & Sword Books Ltd incorporates the imprints of Pen & Sword Archaeology,
Atlas, Aviation, Battleground, Discovery, Family History, History, Maritime, Military,
Naval, Politics, Railways, Select, Social History, Transport, True Crime, Claymore
Press, Frontline Books, Leo Cooper, Praetorian Press, Remember When, Seaforth
Publishing and Wharncliffe.

For a complete list of Pen & Sword titles please contact
Pen & Sword Books Limited
47 Church Street, Barnsley, South Yorkshire, S70 2AS, England
E-mail: enquiries@pen-and-sword.co.uk
Website: www.pen-and-sword.co.uk

Contents

Introduction
Hitler's Problem Child

The Panther tank represented Hitler's 'great white hope', born out of necessity in the harsh Russian winter of 1941. Hitler's key panzer expert Heinz Guderian had swiftly identified the danger facing the German Army; it needed an answer to Mikhail Koshkin's utilitarian T-34 tank. While most of the Rec Army's tank designs had been easily overcome in the summer of 1941, it was the T-34 that represented the biggest long-term threat to Hitler's panzer forces.

Although the T-34 was almost strangled at birth by competing interests among the Soviet defence industries and was less than successful when it first deployed, Guderian appreciated that Hitler needed to counter this revolutionary tank quickly. However, it took German industry a year and a half to produce the Panther and then it fell foul of unending teething problems. Damningly, Guderian was to dub it our 'problem child.' Despite Guderian's best efforts to ensure the crews were fully proficient and the snags were resolved, Hitler insisted the Panther be thrown into battle immediately.

This decision was foolhardy as there were insufficient numbers to make a decisive impact at the Battle of Kursk. The decision to commit both the Panther and its heavier cousin the Tiger in penny packets was a tactical and strategic disaster. The Panther did not cover itself in glory at Kursk, instead continually breaking down, while its inexperienced crews were repeatedly ambushed in the opening days of the battle. Nonetheless, once fine-tuned it proved a worthy adversary on the Eastern Front, in Italy and in Normandy.

Guderian, in his memoirs *Panzer Leader,* recalled how he set off the chain of events that led to the Panther:

Numerous Russian T-34s went into action and inflicted heavy losses on the German tanks at Mzensk in 1941. Up to this time we had enjoyed tank superiority, but from now on the situation was reversed. The prospect of rapid decisive victories was fading in consequence. I made a report on this situation, which was for us a new one, and sent it to the Army Group; in this report I described in plain terms the marked superiority of the T-34 to our PzKpfw IV and drew the relevant conclusion as that must affect our future tank production.

This abrupt and unwelcome reversal of the panzers' superiority, thanks to the unexpected appearance of the T-34, forced the German Army Staff out of its complacency about the performance of the Panzer Mk IV medium tank. Although the panzers had already come up against the T-34, during the summer it had suffered severe transmission problems, carried insufficient ammunition and had poorly trained crews who simply panicked. By the winter these shortcomings had been largely overcome.

It soon became apparent that the panzers were unable to cope with the mud, snow and ice. The panzers, like their Soviet counterparts, had quite narrow tracks that struggled with adverse conditions. The T-34's tracks were much wider, spreading the weight of the tank and giving it much better cross-country performance, especially in bad weather. Guderian took immediate action:

> I concluded by urging a commission to be sent immediately to my sector of the front, and that it should consist of representatives of the Army Ordnance, the Armaments Ministry, the tank designers, and the firms that built tanks. If this commission was on the spot it could not only examine the destroyed tanks on the battlefield, but could also be advised by the men who had used them as to what should be included in the design for our new tanks. I also requested the rapid production of a heavy anti-tank gun with sufficient penetrating power to knock out the T-34. The commission appeared on the Second Panzer Army's front on 20 November 1941.

The commission worked quickly, investigating the key design features of the 30-ton T-34. These in fact were obvious: the sloping armour that gave a greater shot deflection thereby greatly enhancing the armour; the large simple road wheels and broad tracks which gave a stable and steady ride for the crew; and the overhanging gun where the recoil mechanism was partially outside the turret, which the Germans had always considered impractical for their panzers. Of these three the sloping armour was the most revolutionary element of the design.

The German Armaments Ministry was quick to act and on 25 November 1941 instructed the companies of Daimler-Benz and Maschinenfabrik Augsburg-Nürnberg (MAN) to produce two competing designs for a new medium tank in the 30-35 ton category under the ordnance designation of VK.3002. This required 60mm of frontal armour and 40mm of side armour, with the front and sides sloped in the same manner as the T-34's hull. Top speed was to be 55km/h (35mph). The assumption that the tank would not exceed 35 tons was to prove to be optimistic.

Insisting that two competing companies produce competing designs showed a complete lack of focus or urgency. Yet time was a luxury that could be ill afforded in light of the titanic struggle being waged on the Eastern Front. Time was of the essence and yet Hitler, as with the development of the Tiger tank, seemed happy to waste precious resources instead of insisting the panzer manufacturers coordinate their efforts.

The two designs were submitted to Heinrich Ernst Kniepkampf and the Waffenprufamt 6 (the German Army's Weapons Department or Heereswaffenamt, responsible for tank and armoured fighting vehicle procurement) in April 1942. Kniepkampf was one of Koshkin's German counterparts; he had been with the Waffenprufamt 6 since 1936 and had worked his way up to chief engineer and designer. Most notably he had previously worked as a designer at MAN, casting doubts over his impartiality.

Kniepkampf was principally responsible for German half-track development and the introduction of interleaved road wheels, torsion bar suspension and the Maybach-Olvar gearbox in the panzers. All of these, while excellently designed, were ultimately overdesigned when it came to the requirements of mass production and the realities of the battlefield. Such was Kniepkampf's influence that he remained in post until almost the end of the war in 1945. This inevitably meant that he played a key role in the development of the Panther.

The two designs were very different. Daimler-Benz gave Guderian exactly what he wanted, which was a shameless copy of the T-34. It had the hull shape of the T-34, with the turret so far forward that the driver had to sit within the turret cage. It also featured jettisonable external rear fuel tanks, replicating those on the T-34, and side hull escape hatches. It also had a rear sprocket drive driven by an MB507 diesel engine, duplicating the T-34 drive and transmission layout. Dual steel road wheels were suspended by leaf springs (a departure from Christie suspension, but simpler and cheaper).

Like the T-34 the Daimler-Benz design meant that the compact engine and transmission sited at the rear ensured the all-important fighting compartment was relatively uncluttered, allowing for structural change or up-gunning. Likewise, a diesel engine would help reduce the danger of fire and compensate for inevitable petrol shortages. Leaf springs were easier to produce than complicated space-consuming torsion bars and the use of all steel wheels would help if there were rubber shortages. From the start Hitler was impressed by the VK.3002 (DB) 'T-34 type' design, though he pressed for the gun to be improved from the 75mm L/48 model to the more powerful L/70.

MAN took a different tack with an original German design that was sophisticated rather than simple. Some might argue that it was overdesigned. Notably it had a much wider and higher hull than the VK.3002 (DB) or the T-34. The turret was set much further back to allow for the overhang created by the long 75mm gun. A torsion bar suspension was employed, with interleaved road wheels, and it was this that gave rise to the hull's much higher profile. In contrast to the DB design MAN proposed employing a gasoline or petrol Maybach HL. 210 V-12 engine with front drive sprockets.

Hitler's personal preference meant that an initial order for 200 VK.3002 (DB) was placed and prototypes went into production. However, the Waffenprufamt 6 'Panther Committee' led by Kniepkampf preferred to play safe with the VK.3002 (MAN) design, as it was far more conventional by German engineering standards and in terms of internal layout. It is also likely that there was an element of national pride at stake – in some quarters copying an enemy tank may have been seen as an admission of design failure and indeed embarrassing.

This put Hitler in a dilemma, as he had previously instructed that when it came to military equipment under no circumstances were two different designs to be produced at the same time. Karl-Otto Saur, deputy to Armaments Industry Minister Albert Speer, argued that a diesel engine would not be ready in time and that the MAN design should be reconsidered. Aluminium shortages certainly posed problems in the development of a diesel engine. Hitler, on 14 May 1942, after comparing the statistics of the MAN and Daimler-Benz designs, decided that in hindsight the MAN version was the superior and would go into production instead. In making this decision Hitler and Kniepkampf arguably did the panzerwaffe a great disservice.

MAN's proposal was accepted six months after the T-34 had first showed its true potential on the battlefield. The company was instructed to produce a mild steel prototype as quickly as possible and the order for 200 DB vehicles was quietly dropped. It was at this point that Kniepkampf took charge of the detailed design work on the MAN vehicle. The first pilot model of the VK.3002 (MAN) was not completed until September 1942 and was tested at Nuremburg in the MAN factory grounds. A second test model was sent to the Heereswaffenamt testing grounds at Kummersdorf for official Army trials.

By this time the Panther's rival, the Tiger, had just come into production, but its shortcomings in terms of excessive weight, low speed and poor ballistic shape would soon become apparent following its combat debut in North Africa and on the Eastern Front. The Tiger's slow production rate was a real cause for concern, leaving the Army reliant on the tried and tested Panzer Mk IV. As a result the VK.3002 (MAN) was ordered into immediate production as the PzKpfw V Panther with the German ordnance designation of SdKfz 171 (*sonderkraftfahrzeug* – special purpose vehicle).

Hitler stipulated that the glacis plate armour be increased from 60mm to 80mm, increasing the Panther's weight to 45 tons. In contrast the Panzer Mk IV was only around 25 tons. He also instructed that an air-cooled diesel tank engine be given priority, but Speer and Kniepkampf chose to ignore him.

The first production Panther rolled out of MAN in November 1942, exactly a year after the fateful clashes with the T-34 at Mzensk. Originally it was intended that 250 tanks per month would be produced, but at the end of 1942 this was increased to 600. MAN was unable to do this alone, so a Panther production group was formed with the other tank manufacturers. Daimler-Benz was instructed to abandon its almost completed prototypes and switch to the MAN design. They began retooling to build the Panther, with the first DB-produced vehicle appearing in early 1943. In the meantime the German Army suffered a catastrophic defeat at Stalingrad. This left Hitler's aspirations on the Eastern Front hanging in the balance.

In January 1943 Hanover-based Marienfelde Maschinenfabrik Niedersachsen (MNH) and Tiger manufacturer Henschel in Kassel were instructed to start tooling for Panther production. Numerous subcontractors were also involved, making the Panther one of the most concentrated German armament programmes of the Second World War. Even the Luftwaffe felt the squeeze as aircraft production was cut back to free up manufacturing facilities for Panther engines and subcomponents and to conserve fuel for use in the panzers. The next stop for the Panther was Kursk and controversy.

An American M8 Gun Motor Carriage rumbles past a poorly camouflaged Panther belonging to the Panzer Lehr Division, St Gilles, France, July 1944. Fortunately for the Allies this division commenced the Battle for Normandy with its Panther tank battalion strung out between the French capital Paris and the German city of Magdeburg.

Photograph Sources

The photos in this book are drawn from the Canadian National Archives, US Army Archive sources, the Scott Pick collection and the author's own collection, built up over the past 30 years. Inevitably the quality of the images varies, and some of the poorer quality ones have been included for their novelty or uniqueness.

The Ausf D Panther, with its distinctive vertical 'dustbin' turret cupola, got off to a very poor start. Operational reliability rates were to plague the Panther throughout its combat career.

Chapter One

Poor Start – Ausf D

The initial model of the Panther, known as the Panzerkampfwagen V Ausf D (Sd Kfz 171), went into full-scale production in January 1943. The first 20 pre-production models to come off the MAN factory line from November 1942 were designated in the normal German manner as the Ausf A (*Ausführung* – meaning mark or model), but this was later changed to D1.

It was planned that the ZF type AK7-200 gearbox would be replaced by the Maybach Olvar eight-speed gearbox to create the Ausf B. This proved unsatisfactory, so the Ausf B designation was skipped, as was the Ausf C, which seems to have remained on the drawing board. Therefore the first full production model became the Ausf D, hence the initial Ausf A being designated D1, with the D sometimes being referred to as the D2. The upshot of this was that the three Panther production models in order of manufacture were designated the Ausf D, A and G respectively.

The Ausf D required five crew: commander, gunner, loader, driver and wireless operator. On first inspection it looked to be a formidable panzer. Developed by Rheinmetall-Borsig, the Panther's 75mm KwK42 L/70 anti-tank gun was designed as a high-velocity weapon capable of cutting through 140mm of plate armour at 1,000 metres. This was mounted in an external, curved gun mantlet that included a coaxial machine-gun. All but the earliest models had the L/70 gun with the double-baffle muzzle brake. In a stand-off fight this weapon was easily able to tackle the armour of the T-34.

The gunner sat in the turret on the left-hand side and was initially provided with an articulated binocular sight (this was later replaced by a monocular sight) He fired the main gun electrically by a trigger fitted on the elevating hand wheel; using a foot switch he also operated the coaxial machine-gun. Either side of the mantlet exposed on the external sides of the turret were three smoke dischargers.

The turret had very distinctive sloped sides and a rounded front covered by a curved cast mantlet. The interior turret cage had a full floor that rotated with the turret. The drive for the hydraulic traverse was taken through the centre of the floor to a gearbox and then to a motor. The commander's station was located to the left rear of the turret, the offset position being due to the length of the gun's breech that all but divided the turret in two. The loader occupied the right-hand side of the turret.

The Ausf D's superstructure and hull comprised a single built-up unit of machineable quality homogeneous armour plate of welded construction. All the main edges of the hull were strengthened by mortised interlocking joints. The front glacis plate, which was angled at 33 degrees to the horizontal to deflect shells upwards clear of the turret mantlet, was 80mm thick on the upper plate and 60mm on the lower. On the initial Ausf D1 this was 60mm and 40mm respectively.

The massive Maybach HL 230 P30 V-12 23-litre engine, producing 700hp at 3000rpm, was located in the rear compartment. This provided a top speed of 46km/h with a range of 200km. Access to the engine was via a large inspection hatch in the centre of the rear decking. The cooling grilles and fans took up most of the remaining rear decking space. The engine on the Ausf D was uprated from the HL 210 P30 installed in the D1.

The hydraulic power takeoff for the turret and gun was connected to the engine by a propeller shaft. This was also connected to the gearbox and the brake/transmission unit in the front of the tank. The Panther, because it was heavier and bulkier than previous panzers, needed a beefed-up gearbox (the Panzer Mk IV, which the Panther was meant to eventually replace, was over 20 tons lighter). Designated the AK 7-200, this was an all synchromesh unit with seven forward and one reverse gear. Argus hydraulic disc brakes provided the steering by braking the tracks. The epicyclic gears also helped steer the Panther by driving one of the sprockets against the main drive: this retarded the track and permitted sharper radius turns.

German engineers usually paid attention to detail, but there were warning signs that the Ausf D was a rushed job. Despite the radical difference in hull shape compared to the previous family of panzers, a number of weaknesses were instantly apparent with both the sloped hull and turret designs.

Notably, there were openings in the turret that weakened the overall integrity of the armour. On the left-hand side was a small ammunition-loading hatch, while at the rear was a crew-access hatch. Both of these presented stress points. Similarly, the front glacis plate had two openings; on the left-hand side the driver was served by an armoured flap with a vision port fitted with a laminated glass screen. Under combat conditions this flap was kept shut and the driver had to rely on two fixed periscopes on the hull roof; one faced directly forward and one half left – as they were fixed this greatly limited the driver's range of view. The wireless operator, who also served as hull machine-gunner, was provided with a primitive vertical opening 'letterbox' flap in the glacis plate on the right, through which he could fire the standard MG 34 machine gun. Understandably, the lack of a ball mount for the machine gun greatly restricted its utility when engaging the enemy.

While the Panther turret was well armoured and angled to deflect shot, its size and height presented a welcome target for enemy gunners. In addition, the front mantlet was found to deflect shot into the thinly armoured hull roof. The latter problem was not fully addressed until the third model of Panther tank. On the T-34 the turret's rear overhand created a shot trap that caused a similar problem.

Access to the turret could also be gained via the cupola hatch that pivoted to the side. Due to its prominent vertical shape it was known as the 'dustbin' cupola, and featured six vision slits that offered poor visibility. The pivoting driver and radio-operator hatches were far from ideal and it was soon discovered that they jammed easily if debris caught in the hinges.

The Panther's suspension comprised eight pairs of large interleaved dished discs with solid rubber-tyre road wheels sprung on torsion bars, a front drive sprocket and rear idler. The first, third, fifth and seventh road wheels from the front were double, with the intervening axles carrying the spaced wheels overlapping the others on the inside and outside. Each bogie axle was joined by a radius arm to a torsion bar coupled in series to a second bar lying parallel to it.

The suspension, while technically advanced and giving excellent floatation, was hellishly difficult to maintain because of the size of the wheels and the inaccessibility of the axles and torsion bars. Replacing the heavy road wheels was a time-consuming task and the number of wheel-rim bolts proved insufficient and led to failures. The lack of track covers also left the tracks vulnerable to anti-tank weapons.

In summary, the key distinctive characteristics of the model D Panther were the 'dustbin' cupola, the vision port and machine-gun port on the glacis, smoke dischargers on the turret sides, plus a straight edge to the lower sponson sides with separate storage bins fabricated beneath the rear ends. Towards the end of the Ausf D production run an improved cupola was installed and the smoke dischargers were dispensed with and replaced by an anti-personnel bomb thrower fitted in the turret roof and operated by the loader. In addition some later D models were fitted with side-skirt armour to protect the upper track run. Textured Zimmerit anti-magnetic paste was also applied to prevent the attachment of mines.

From January to September 1943 MAN, Daimler-Benz, MNH and Henschel built a total of 850 Ausf D. At an average of about 100 a month this was a pitifully low rate of production. The first vehicles were sent to their units in February, but in April the process was halted after those issued were recalled for major modifications. During the summer and following the Panther's performance at Kursk it became evident that a new production model was required to remedy the Panther's existing shortcomings. This led, somewhat confusingly, to the Ausf A.

The Maschinenfabrik Augsburg Nürnberg-designed Panther Ausf D initially went into production in November 1942. The following year half a dozen other companies became involved. This factory is building model D hulls. Slow output, plus mechanical problems, requiring the initial batch to be returned to the factory and crew training requirements delayed Hitler's 1943 summer offensive by almost two months. This gave the Red Army ample time to build up its defences in the Kursk salient.

Brand new Ausf Ds about to be shipped to their units. The prominent 'dustbin' cupola, the letterbox flap for the hull gunner and driver's hatch are all clearly visible. The mantlet features a single opening for the coaxial machine gun and small twin openings for the gunner's binocular scope.

More Ausf Ds being transported to the front – the unreliability of their engines and transmissions left them vulnerable to air attack when being moved on railcars. These tanks, like the previous ones, sport the factory finish *dunkel gelb* (deep sand-yellow).

This Ausf D was photographed in Germany and gives a good view of the glacis plate – the armour was 80mm on the upper plate and 60mm on the lower. It has two prominent headlamps fitted with blackout covers.

After the Ausf D was issued to the initial training units it had to be sent back because of its unreliability. Note the access hatch in the rear of the turret and the equipment boxes fitted each side of the rear hull plate. They have all armoured side-skirts protecting the upper tracks.

The exposed and therefore vulnerable Ausf D 'dustbin' cupola had six vision ports that provided poor visibility for the commander. It was replaced on the subsequent models with a lower and more angular cupola.

The Panther's interleaved wheels, while giving good stability, were difficult to maintain – in addition there were insufficient rim bolts on the Ausf D wheels that led to stress failures.

The subsequent Ausf A and G models featured double the number of wheel rim bolts. The front drive sprocket was of a similar design used on all panzers and could be easily damaged by shellfire. This Ausf G belonged to Panzer Brigade 106 and was abandoned west of Metz in the summer of 1944.

A partially camouflaged Ausf G photographed in France, August 1944. The passing civilian gives some idea of the imposing and intimidating bulk of the Panther. Fritz Bayerlein, commander of Panzer Lehr Division, was of the view the Panther was ill-suited for the conditions in Normandy.

The Panther featured twin rear exhausts. The hatches on the back plate gave access to the engine compartment for the inertia starter and track tensioners.

This first production version Ausf D or Model D Panther was captured in the Rhineland in 1945. It was probably a rebuild from earlier battles. There is no visible battle damage and the engine cover to the rear is raised, suggesting it was abandoned. The tank's distinctive outline was partially obscured by the addition of local foliage.

Chapter Two

Combat Improvements – Ausf A

Just as the Panther was making its appearance, General Heinz Guderian was appointed Inspector-General of armoured troops in February 1943, reporting directly to Adolf Hitler. He found himself with responsibility for almost all armoured units in the German Army, Waffen-SS and the Luftwaffe – the artillery, however, would not relinquish control of their assault guns thanks to the wording of Guderian's terms of reference.

Guderian was not happy with the Panther Ausf D and indeed tried to delay it being sent to the Eastern Front. 'I spent June 15th [1943] worrying about our problem child, the Panther,' he recalled, 'the track suspension and drive were not right and the optics were also not yet satisfactory. On the next day I told Hitler of my reasons for not wishing to see the Panthers sent into action in the East. They were simply not yet ready to go to the front.'

Hitler would not listen, and the 'problem child' was sent to Kursk and suffered as a result. The very hard-won lessons involving the Ausf D at the Battle of Kursk were soon learned and put into practice. Confusingly, the second production model of the Panther, which appeared in August 1943, was designated the Ausf A rather than the Ausf E, as might have been expected. While the basic design remained the same as the initial Ausf D, it featured a series of detailed modifications that attempted to improve the Panther's troublesome performance.

The Ausf A was fractionally larger than the D. The hull armour was unchanged, but the turret was up-armoured at the front by an extra 10mm, giving it 110mm, while the sides and rear remained 40mm and the roof just 16mm. Although the hull was the same, a new machine-gun ball mount was installed to replace the clumsy letterbox flap. This had proved far from ideal in the heat of battle and could allow enemy infantry to fire into the interior of the tank. The upgrade was not immediate, as the ball mounts were initially only fitted to a proportion of Ausf A, although they were eventually installed in all Ausf A from the close of the year. Likewise the gunner's TZF12 binocular-sighting telescope was gradually replaced by improved the monocular TZF12A.

The turret received many minor modifications that included a new cupola with seven equally-spaced armoured periscopes and a semi-circular rail to mount an MG34 machine gun for air defence. This was tacit acknowledgement after Kursk that perhaps the Red Air Force had not been defeated after all. The later-type cupola fitted to the Ausf A (and subsequent Ausf G) was machined from a homogeneous armour casting. The mountings for the episcope blocks were welded onto the casting. The new cupola hatch opened vertically. To simplify turret production and strengthen the armour the side pistol ports and small loading hatch of the Ausf D were dispensed with, leaving just the big round escape/loading hatch in the turret rear. This also served to improve the integrity of the turret armour.

As long as the turret could rotate, the coaxial machine gun was normally the best method for keeping enemy infantry at bay, along with the hull-mounted machine gun. While turret pistol ports were common, they were a crude means of coping with close-quarter fighting in the event of enemy infantry clambering over a tank's hull. On the Ausf D they consisted of an opening on either side of the turret that could be sealed by a steel bung held in place by a chain (a similar arrangement was used on the later T-34). The crew could fire handguns or machine pistols out of the port either blind or using the vision blocks in the cupola.

Clearly the pistol ports were rather hit and miss when it came to defending the tank. On the Ausf A the pistol ports were swapped in favour of the much more effective *Nahverteidigungswaffe,* or close-in defence weapon, mounted in the roof. This was designed to disperse smoke and the crew could fire a flare pistol through it. The pistol could discharge smoke rounds, flares and small-calibre fragmentation grenades. The latter had the advantage of keeping enemy infantry away from the tank before they ever closed in.

A number of modifications were made to the drive train and engine cooling to improve reliability and the number of wheel rim bolts was doubled. On the Ausf D the heads had a habit of shearing off when placed under excessive stress. Side-skirts of 5mm armour and the Zimmerit paste coating were standardised. However, the skirt fittings were not terribly robust and tended to get torn off in combat or simply be removed by the crews. These changes caused a slight increase in weight: whereas the Ausf D came in at about 43 tons, the Ausf A weighed almost 45 tons, although this made no discernible difference to its performance.

The Ausf A proved far more successful than the initial model, with double the production. From August 1943 to May 1944 Hitler's panzer factories, run by Daimler-Benz, Henschel, MAN and MNH, produced 2,000 tanks. These saw action on the Eastern Front and in Italy. In addition the Panther Ausf A was the principal type of Panther deployed to counter the Allied invasion of Normandy. Unfortunately for the Panther, in many instances geographical conditions did not favour its key asset.

The second model of Panther, known as the Ausf A, went into production in August 1943, drawing on lessons learned at the Battle of Kursk. Improvements included a new lower cupola fitted with a rail mount for an anti-aircraft machine gun. This example has been coated with Zimmerit anti-magnetic paste, which was applied in the factories before painting from early 1943 onwards. Normally a spreader gave it a horizontal ridged pattern, but a number of criss-cross patterns with vertical ridges were used on the Panther.

The crew of this Ausf A has up-armoured the turret with spare track links. Normally on all models of Panther spare track links were carried on mounting racks at the rear on both sides of the hull. The A and G models were only provided with a single headlamp on the left. The metal tube on the side of the hull holds the gun-cleaning equipment.

On the Ausf A the clumsy letterbox port on the right was replaced by a machine-gun ball mount. Initially this upgrade was only fitted to a proportion of new Panthers, but was standardised from late 1943. This particular Ausf A was knocked out during the fighting in Normandy in the summer of 1944. It has a very crude criss-cross finish to the Zimmerit on the glacis and from the pattern on the barrel has clearly been painted in a camouflage scheme.

Two more Panthers lost in the fighting in France. The nearest one has been placed in a hull-down position and then camouflaged.

Allied air superiority over Normandy meant the Panthers often had to move and fight heavily camouflaged. These two Ausf A belonged to the Panzer Lehr Division and appear to have been abandoned.

This Normandy Panther has its rear turret access hatch open. On the Ausf A the turret pistol ports and small loading hatch were dispensed with.

These two Panthers captured in Normandy have the newer-type cupola fitted to the Ausf A and G models. Brackets welded to the episcope block housing on top of the cupola supported the machine-gun mount. Also visible on the turret roof is the circular cover of the extractor fan and the turret lifting rings fitted just behind the mantlet. The cupola hatch is missing on the nearest tank. The pivoted driver's hatch visible on the second tank was standard on the D and A models but replaced on the G.

A Panther Ausf A in Zimmerit with a sand-yellow and olive green sprayed pattern. The German national black cross edged with white has been applied to the rear and the extreme front end of the hull side.

The bulk of the Ausf A, which was slightly larger than the D, meant that it was difficult to manoeuvre in tight confines, as in this town.

Chapter Three

Third Time Lucky – Ausf G

The Ausf G was the third in the Panther series, drawing on combat recommendations from the panzer crews in the field who had fought with the Ausf D and A. Not surprisingly the panzertruppen had been quick to identify the earlier models' shortcomings. The main difference in the G model was a redesigned hull, which featured an increase in the side armour on the upper hull side. The side was formed from a single plate. Soviet tank crews had swiftly learned at Kursk that the best way to kill a Panther was from the side, and preferably from a hull-down position. Penetrating the Panther's glacis plate was almost impossible except at short range.

Visually the most immediate change was the removal of the driver's vision port from the glacis plate to improve the integrity of the armour. The driver now steered either with his head poking out of the hatch courtesy of a seat that could be raised, or, if closed up, by employing a rotating periscope. The driver and radio operator's pivoting access hatches were replaced by hinged ones to improve reliability. If the crew had to bail out in a hurry, the last thing they wanted was a hatch that jammed at the critical moment.

Efforts were made once again to tackle the vexed issue of dependability, most notably with the overstressed drive train. An oil cooler was also installed with the gearbox to improve performance. The suspension remained the same, though in some later production vehicles the rearmost hydraulic dampers were deleted. In September 1944 a trial production series was fitted with steel-rimmed 'silent bloc' wheels that were also to be standard on the aborted Panther Ausf F.

At the same time, some turrets were fitted with a new gun mantlet that had the under curve eliminated; this was designed to stop hits being deflected into the thin hull roof armour. This improvement showed that the problem was commonplace enough to need remedying. Again at Kursk Soviet anti-tank gunners had been able to get above the Ausf D and shoot down into the upper hull. The cupola on the late Ausf G, as on the Ausf A, had Ersatzgläser blocks held in place by a simple springlock mechanism. This allowed any blocks damaged by shell splinters to be quickly replaced.

As with the Ausf A, the G was equipped with the TZF12A monocular sight marked with range scales for all types of ammunition carried, with the high explosive scale also being used for aiming the machine gun. A total of 79 main armament rounds were carried in the Ausf A and D. This increased to 82 in the G, which were stowed in racks and lockers in the lower half of the fighting compartment. Up to 5,100 rounds of MG34 ammunition were carried in the first two models and 4,800 in the Ausf G.

In the name of crew comfort, from October 1944 the fighting compartment was belatedly fitted with a dedicated heating system that drew warm air from a tower-like device installed over the left-hand side engine fan. On the Eastern Front such a mechanism was vital during the bitter winters. These various improvements to the Ausf G again meant an inevitable slight increase in weight over the Ausf D, with the new Panther weighing in at 45.5 tons.

Although the introduction of the Ausf G did fix many of the persistent problems that had beset the early Ausf D and A, such as the engine fires and weak drives, the Panther remained a gas-guzzler and by mid-1944 was increasingly vulnerable to Soviet 85mm and 122mm tank guns. Nonetheless, the Ausf G proved to be the most numerous Panther, with 3,126 built from March 1944 to April 1945. This type served on both the Eastern and Western Fronts and saw combat with Hitler's last offensives in East Prussia, Hungary and Belgium. Ultimately, though, the Ausf G proved too few too late by this stage of the conflict.

Panther construction continued until the end of the war and was expanded beyond the Panther group of MAN, Daimler-Benz, Demag, Henschel, MNH and MIAG (the main gun was built by Rheinmetal Borsig of Berlin-Tegel). Use was also made of three key steelworks in Polish Upper Silesia: Bankhütte was involved in engineering and hull/superstructure fabrication and Bismarckhütte and Konigshütte produced electric steel. Although the MNH Panther factory at Hanover was severely damaged several times by Allied bombing, quantities of Ausf G and Jagdpanther components, including turret hulls and superstructures, were found to be largely intact when it was finally captured.

The immediate visual difference on the Panther Ausf G was the removal of the driver's port from the glacis plate. Note the impact marks on the mantlet to the right of the barrel.

This Ausf G was captured by the Americans after an explosion ripped open its right-hand side. The rubber tyres have been peeled off the road wheels by the blast and the track severed.

This severely battle-damaged Ausf G had its tracks, outer road wheels and idler removed for transport. The right-hand drive sprocket also appears to be missing. The turret is twisted off and has lifted up from the hull. Note the single circular opening visible on the mantlet for the TZF12 gunner's sight.

This Ausf G of SS-Panzer Regiment 1 has the September 1944 modification to the lower edge of the gun mantlet, which eliminated the under curve in an attempt to stop shot being deflected into the hull roof. It was photographed in the Ardennes in January 1945.

Another captured Ausf G – the hull and turret are coated in the Zimmerit anti-magnetic paste. There is also evidence that the tank was painted in a camouflage scheme.

This late-model Ausf G has the forward angled protection on the lower edge of the gun mantlet. Both drive sprockets have been damaged rendering the tank immobile. Likewise the top of the turret has suffered damage.

This Panther Ausf G was photographed near Cleryaux, Luxembourg, in February 1945. The absence of Zimmerit paste shows that it was from the final production runs. It appears to have been sprayed in olive green and sand-yellow. The gloss effect is presumably due to the rain. The starter handle at the rear suggests it broke down and refused to start.

This Ausf G was abandoned and then shunted off the road. It appears to be painted in a disruptive camouflage scheme.

Chapter Four

Stillborn – Ausf F and Panther II

The final Panther designed by Daimler-Benz never went into production, though at least one prototype was completed, along with eight hulls, n 1945. In an attempt to counter shot penetration under the wide gun mantlet it was decided to reduce the turret's frontal area while still having the same size turret ring. Daimler-Benz was instructed to produce a 'Schmal' or narrow Panther turret that could be installed on the proposed Ausf F and the Panther II. This move belatedly acknowledged the superiority of the narrow fronted T-34 turret. It also indicates that the modifications to the curved lower edge of the mantlet on the Ausf G were not entirely successful. In fact, the flat front may have aggravated the problem. The Panther's turret front presented a large target and numerous Panthers were photographed with shot damage and penetration holes on the mantlet. Even if the enemy rounds did not cut through the armour plate, the resulting shrapnel could damage the turret traverse, the barrel and the hull hatches.

Dr Wunderlich, assisted by Waffenprufamt 6 gunnery expert Colonel Henrici, directed the new turret development. This proved to be successful; although it had the same ring diameter as the old turret, it had 30 per cent more armour plate and took 30 per cent less time to build. A single prototype turret armed with the KwK42/1 L/70 was produced and there were plans to develop mounts that could take a proposed lengthened L/100 version of the same weapon and the powerful 88mm KwK with a stabilized sight. The gun mantlet was conical (known as *Saukopf,* or pig's head) with range-finder bulges in the turret sides.

Other changes included increasing the hull roof armour from 16mm to 25mm. This was a shortcoming in all three models of Panther. For reasons that are not entirely clear, the hull machine-gun mount was designed to take the MP44 assault rifle rather than the normal machine gun. The Ausf F was also designed so that it could be easily converted to a command tank in the field. Despite these alterations the tank weighed 45 tons.

It seems that this new model was a perfected version of the original Ausf D. Certainly it would have been a better weapon of war than the bulky 68-ton Tiger II. However, the Ausf F was never mass-produced, as conditions dictated that Hitler's panzer factories had to press on producing already-proven panzers such as the Mk IV. In addition, it was probably felt that there was little point in continuing with the Ausf F when the Panther II was already on the drawing board.

Once the Tiger and Panther tanks were in production, German designers began to plan for a new generation of panzers that could draw on lessons learned from all the existing designs. In light of the heavy fighting on the Eastern Front, reducing maintenance, economizing on materials and simplifying production became paramount. In addition, a key request from the panzertruppen and their mechanics was for components to be standardized as much as possible. This reduced the need for large stocks of differing spare parts and would greatly speed up getting repaired panzers back into the field.

In February 1943 Waffenprufamt 6 instructed MAN and Henschel to come up with improvements for the Panther and the Tiger, ensuring interchangeability of parts. At the time the main priority was finding a replacement for the less-than-perfect and very expensive Tiger, so Henschel pushed ahead with the Tiger II, or King Tiger, which went into production at the end of 1943. Kniepkampf was in overall charge of both the Tiger II and the improved Panther projects.

In the meantime, the enhanced Panther or Panther II was to have a similar hull to the existing Panther, but use the same interleaved all-steel resilient wheels as the Tiger II. It was to feature an improved gearbox and transmission; the AK7-400 and the mechanical parts, including brakes, were identical to those of the Tiger II. The hull-top armour was doubled to 25mm and the ball mount was altered to take the MG42.

Plans for the Panther's successor envisaged an up-armoured 47-ton variant with 100mm frontal armour and 60mm side armour. The Panther II design was conducted alongside the Tiger II, which led to unwelcome delays with the latter. The need to produce as many Panther Ausf G as possible meant that the Panther II was not seen as a priority, but two prototypes were ordered in 1944 and one, featuring a Panther I turret, was delivered by MAN in 1945. At 55 tons its running gear utilized the steel-rimmed wheels, drive and idler sprockets of the Tiger II. It featured only seven wheel stations either side. However, by the time the war ended the Panther II design had already been superseded by the E-50 and E-75 tank projects.

For the Panther II chassis a panzerjäger self-propelled variant was proposed using a massive 128mm gun, the argest possible weapon that could be installed on the chassis. Gerät 5-12 was Krupp's design for a 12.8cm K43 on the Panther chassis, while Gerät 5-1213 was Rheinmetall's design for the same weapon on the Panther. Neither of these got beyond the drawing board stage and their existence shows that Hitler was happy to let his designers waste time and resources dreaming up new flights of fancy.

This shot gives a good indication of the overlapping design of the eight double interleaved rubber-rimmed steel road wheels. The Panther employed a slack track method using no return rollers for the upper track – similar to the T-34. Note how the front drive sprocket's teeth engage the steel track links.

This close-up shows the pin method used to connect the track links. The tracks are 65cm wide with 86 links on the D, and 66cm with 87 links on the A and G models. Grousers could be fitted on every fifth link to improve traction in adverse conditions.

The rubber-rimmed road wheels are solid discs. These enhanced the armour of the lower hull by protecting it against lateral shots.

The Ausf G mantlet showing the opening for the coaxial machine gun.

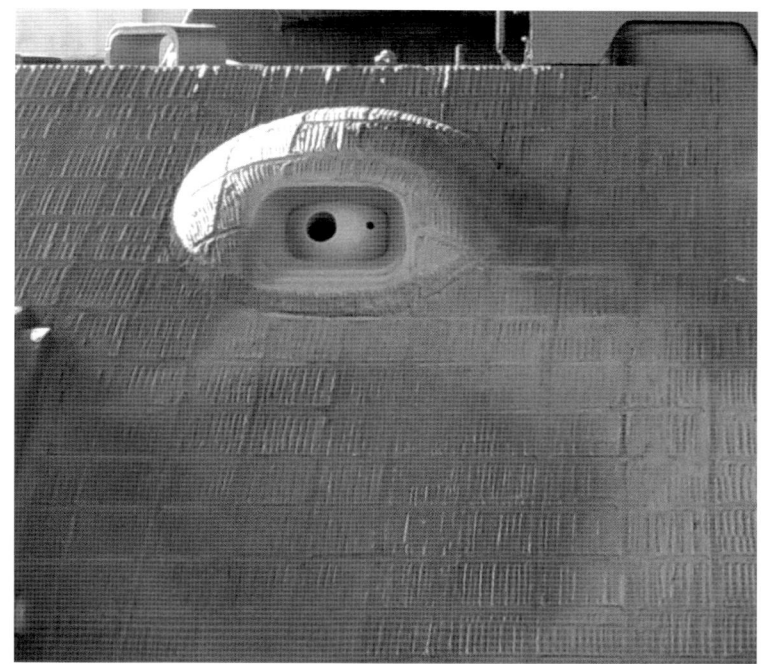

Front of the hull showing the ball mount for the hull machine gun on the A and G models. The Panther was armed with the MG34 in the hull and the turret.

This model Panther Ausf F illustrates the proposed *Schmal* or narrow turret. This fourth type of gun tank Panther never went into production. Likewise, the Panther II, which was intended to be compatible with the Tiger II, never saw the light of day.

This Ausf A was knocked out in Normandy during Operation Epsom on 27 June 1944. As there are no signs of damage and the driver and hull gunner's hatches are open, it may well have been abandoned by its crew.

Judging by the damage to this Ausf A or G's gun mantlet a shot was deflected into the driver's compartment, tearing off his hatch.

This burnt out Panther Ausf G was lost during the Battle of the Bulge in December 1944. All the hatches are open, indicating that the crew fled.

This Ausf G belonging to 9th Panzer was destroyed outside Cologne Cathedral in early March 1945.

This Panther was destroyed whilst operating from an ambush position – like most tanks the Panther was not suited to close-quarter urban combat.

Chapter Five

Panther Variants

The Panther tank chassis was intended to provide the basis for a whole range of armoured fighting vehicles that would include command, flak, self-propelled gun and recovery variants. Very few of these got any further than the proposal or design stage, as time simply ran out in the closing months of the war. Ultimately only the command, armoured recovery and tank hunter versions were produced in any notable numbers to serve alongside the gun tanks.

Panther Armoured Recovery Vehicle

Major problems recovering the 57-ton Tiger from late 1942 meant a dedicated Panther recovery vehicle was vital. This was needed to replace the 18-ton half-track in the heavy recovery role, as it took up to three of these to shift heavy tanks such as the Tiger and the Panther.

In June 1943 the first 12 Panzer-Bergegerät Panther I Sd Kfz 179s, better known as Bergepanthers, were produced by MAN using a Ausf D turretless chassis. This was little more than a towing vehicle, with a limited superstructure consisting of heavy wooden cladding over a mild steel frame built round the former turret opening. The following month Henschel commenced building 70 Bergepanthers from the Ausf D before the company stopped Panther production altogether in November 1943. These were equipped with a 40-ton winch, spade and 1.5-ton derrick.

The requirement for Panther armoured recovery vehicles was not fully met and in February 1944 the manufacturers Demag converted their entire production line over to Bergepanthers. This time they utilized the Panther Ausf A chassis with the letterbox machine-gun port still in the hull front plate. An additional 150 Ausf A variants were built until the G variant went into production. Armament consisted of two MG34 machine guns mounted on a gun shield at the front of the hull and the early Ausf A Bergepanthers included the 20mm KwK38 gun.

Hitler, perhaps not wishing to detract from Panther gun tank production, ordered that all subsequent recovery vehicles be constructed from existing Panthers sent for rebuilds. It was planned that 13 Bergepanthers would be provided in April 1944, followed by 18 in May, 20 in June and 10 in July. This schedule was never met and only eight conversions were managed in August 1944. In total 232 Bergepanthers were produced from June 1943 to September 1944, using the Ausf A plus the eight conversions. Then from September 1944 to March 1945 Demag produced 107 Ausf G versions.

Panther Ammunition Carriers

Some Bergepanthers without spades later had their winches removed and were converted into Munitionpanzer Panthers to carry ammunition for the gun tanks. Other existing Panthers simply had their turrets removed and were also used as munitions carriers. These were ad hoc field modifications and were not put into formal factory production. Externally they looked the same as the Bergepanther, minus the winch gear.

Assault Panther

Plans for an assault variant, or Sturmpanther, began in late 1944 with a view to mounting a 150mm StuH43/1 gun on the chassis. This, however, never went into production. Designs were also produced for a Waffenträger, or weapons carrier, based on the Panther with a turret-mounted 105mm LeFH howitzer.

Panther Command Tank

Two versions of the Panther command/observation tank were produced; the former retained the 75mm gun while the latter did not. The trick with command tanks, which carried more radio equipment than usual, was to make them as inconspicuous as possible or they immediately attracted enemy fire. Deployed by regimental and battalion commanders, as well as staff officers, Befehlswagen Panthers could only be distinguished externally by the extra aerials or the call sign number when visible.

The Panzerbefehlswagen with 7.5cm KwK42 L/70 had an FuG5 radio installed in the turret and an FuG7 or FuG8 radio positioned in the hull over the gearbox. This Pz Bef Wg was fitted with two additional radio aerials, comprising a 1.4m rod on the right side of the turret and a star aerial in the centre rear of the engine deck.

For designation purposes there were two externally similar models of Panther command tank, differing only in the radio installation. The Sd Kfz 267 had the FuG5 and FuG8, while the Sd Kfz 268 had the FuG5 and FuG7. In each type ammunition stowage was reduced from 79 to 64 75mm tank gun rounds. In total 329 Panthers were converted to a command role from May 1943 to February 1945.

Panther Observation Tank

The much rarer observation Panther, designated the Panzerbeobachtungswagen Sd Kfz 172, was produced by converting rebuilt Panthers in late 1944. Old Ausf Ds were used to create observation-post vehicles for operations officers, commanders and staff officers of the self-propelled artillery regiments. To create space for the Blockstelle 0 range-plotting table and other instrumentation for artillery observation the 75mm gun was removed, the front plated over and the turret fixed in place. Instead a dummy gun was installed to give the illusion of a gun tank, to the right of which was fitted a ball-mounted machine gun to provide some close-in protection. New front plate flaps covered the openings for an EM 1.25m R (Pz) stereoscopic range-finder. Like the command tank, the observation variant was also fitted with two additional radio aerials. Just 41 observation Panthers were produced by the end of the war.

Flak Panther

Rheinmetall-Borsig started creating a flak panzer version of the Panther in December 1943 by mounting twin 37mm FlaK43 anti-aircraft guns in a fully armoured turret on an Ausf D chassis. A wooden mock-up was produced and fitted to a hull, but actual production never came to fruition. Other designs included a mount for the 88mm FlaK41 on the Panther chassis.

Infra-red Panther

In late 1944 a number of Panthers were experimentally fitted with night-fighting infra-red equipment with a range of 400m. The Sd Kfz 251/20 half-track, known as the Infrarotscheinwerfer or UHU (Eagle Owl), was introduced as the command and observation vehicle for five-tank strong infra-red Panther platoons. The UHU, equipped with a 60cm Beobachtungs Gerät 1251 infra-red searchlight and Beobachtungs Gerät 1221 telescope, could illuminate and sight targets out to 1,500m. The UHU commander would then direct the Panthers on to their targets using the FuG5 radio, once they had closed to some 500m. Although 600 Eagle Owls were ordered in August 1944, only 60 were ever delivered. Likewise, the number of infra-red Panthers was limited. Some were used during Hitler's Ardennes offensive.

Jagdpanther

Undoubtedly the most successful and deadly of the Panther variants was the heavy tank destroyer or Jagdpanther Sd Kfz 173, also longwindedly known as the Panzerjäger für 8.8cm PaK43 auf Fgst Panther I. This fitted the powerful 88mm PaK4/3 L/71 anti-tank gun into the Panther hull. Earlier attempts to produce a heavy tank destroyer had largely been unsuccessful, and in some cases were little more than bodge jobs. The 88mm anti-tank gun had already been mounted in the Porsche-designed Tiger I chassis to create limited numbers of the Ferdinand, and it had also been installed on the Panzer Mk III/IV chassis as the Nashorn. Both improvisations had proven unsatisfactory – the Ferdinand was far too heavy and lacked protection against enemy infantry, while the Nashhorn was too small and underpowered.

The order for Jagdpanther development was issued on 2 October 1942 and a wooden mock-up was completed the following October. This was shown to Hitler on 16 December 1943 anc he liked what he saw. To house the 88mm gun a fighting compartment was created by removing the Panther turret and extending the upper hull and side plates to make a well-sloped enclosed superstructure. Armour was 80mm on the front and 60mm at the sides. The suspension used was that of the Panther, although the drive train was upgraded with the installation of a heavy-duty transmission to cope with the slight weight increase.

The L/71 was installed in a mount in the sloping front plate of the new superstructure. On the early models the gun mount was welded into place, while on the later ones it was bolted. The first production models had a monobloc or single-piece gun barrel, while the middle and late production vehicles had a distinctive two-piece barrel.

The driver operated via a periscope in the superstructure next to the gun mount and two hull vision slots (reduced to one in later models). The rest of the five-man crew were served by periscopes in the superstructure roof. Close defence was provided by a machine gun to the right of the main armament, plus the *Nahverteidigungsgerät* close defence weapon mounted in the roof.

Production of the Jagdpanther commenced at MIAG in January 1944, at MNH in November 1944 and continued until the end of the war. The intention was to build 150 per month, but disrupt on of the production facilities during the last year of the war by Allied bombers made this impossible. Only 392 Jagdpanthers were built: far too few to have anything more than a local impact on the battlefield. The first units to be issued with Jagdpanthers in June 1944 were the 559th and 654th Panzerjägerabteilungen. Only the latter received its full complement of 42 vehicles. The Jagdpanther saw combat in Normandy, the Ardennes and on the Eastern Front.

Panther Tank Destroyer

Towards the end of the war Krupp was working on a prototype rigid-mounted 88mm PaK43/1 L/71 in the Jagdpanther. Prototypes utilizing such rigid mounts in the Jagdpanzer 38(t) showed that the Jagdpanther was more suitable. This vehicle was known as the Jagdpanther Starr, but it never got beyond the prototype stage.

Weapons Carrier Panther

The Geschützwagen Panther für sFH18/4(sf), or weapons carrier variant, was ordered in early 1944 using a shortened Panther suspension. This featured a lifting beam to manoeuvre the 50mm SFH18 howitzer. Daimler-Benz got as far as producing a prototype before the war ended.

The weight of the Panther was such that it needed its own dedicated recovery vehicle, known as the Bergepanther. This shows the dismountable jib in the erected position on an Ausf D chassis.

A large rear spade was fitted to the Bergepanther that could be lowered to anchor the vehicle while carrying out heavy recovery operations.

This Ausf G command tank variant is identifiable by the star aerial mounted in the centre rear of the engine deck. Judging by the impact mark on the mantlet next to the opening for the gunner's sight this Panther has seen some action. There also appears to be damage to the mantlet left of the barrel.

An Ausf G fitted with the infra-red night fighting equipment, which is visible on the top of the cupola. A number of these infra-red Panthers saw combat during the Ardennes offensive. It has been painted in what was dubbed the 'ambush' camouflage scheme.

Children pose on an Ausf A stranded in France. It has thrown a track as the exposed left-hand drive sprocket is clearly visible.

This Jagdpanther has an early production hull featuring the two vision slots for the driver and the welded-on mantlet collar. However, it has the later two-piece L/71 gun barrel. The superstructure is riddled with small impact dents.

The later bolted-on gun mantlet collar was easier to produce and made replacing the gun much easier. Note the 8.8cm PaK43/3 L/71 round in front of the vehicle.

Two Jagdpanthers photographed in Normandy serving with the Schwere Panzerjäger Abteilung 654. Both vehicles appear to have the early welded-on gun mount and are coated in Zimmerit.

This Jagdpanther has had its glacis penetrated. Such a hit would have killed the crew instantly. The track on the right has also been hit. This is a later production model with the bolt-on gun mantlet collar and two-piece barrel.

Chapter Six

Baptism of Fire

In the months preceding the summer of 1943 General Kurt Zeitzler, German Army Chief of Staff, was preoccupied with Operation Citadel. This was a massive and desperate effort to wrestle back the strategic initiative on the Eastern Front following the catastrophic defeat at Stalingrad during the winter of 1942–43. Red Army operations had left them in possession of a vast salient around Kursk, flanked by German re-entrants centred in the south on Kharkov and in the north on Orel. Hitler's intention was to snip off the Soviet salient, trapping the Red Army using all available means. This meant deploying the Panther.

After his appointment as Inspector General of Armoured Troops Guderian visited the Henschel tank works at Kassel, which was producing Tigers and Panthers. He also inspected the Nibelungen works at Linz that were likewise producing Panthers. While impressed by these new panzers he was clearly not impressed by the rate of production, noting 'we can reckon to equipping a limited number of battalions with Panthers and Tigers during 1943, but the Panther battalions at any rate will not be ready for action before July or August.' Such a view was at odds with Hitler's scheduling for Citadel.

At the beginning of the year the very first Panther battalions were established at Grafenwöhr, consisting of the 51st Battalion, based on the 2nd Company, Panzer Regiment 33 from the 9th Panzer Division and the 52nd Battalion based on the 1st Panzer Company, Panzer Regiment 15, 11th Panzer Division. Panther training was undertaken at Erlangen near Grafenwöhr and this was up and running by May 1943. The intention was that it would turn out one trained Panther battalion every month.

The training did not go at all well and set the tone for the Panther's future shambolic performance. While some of the tank gunners were sent to the Putlos gunnery school, training at Erlangen never got above platoon level. This was to have very serious consequences when the Panthers shipped east to Kursk. The battalions' mechanics spent much of their time liasing with MAN engineers trying to iron out the 'problem child's' persistent 'teething problems.' By April everyone admitted defeat and the Ausf Ds were unceremoniously returned to the manufacturers for modification.

The Panther crews now found themselves without tanks, so for some reason it was decided to despatch them to the panzer base at Mailly le Camp in France. They suffered yet more misfortune when the RAF caught them en route at Mannheim, killing four panzertruppen. They did not return to Grafenwöhr until June to be reissued with their Panthers. Nonetheless, problems remained with the steering and transmission (both originally intended for a much lighter tank). The engine was still overloaded, and once overheated could and did catch fire. This problem was aggravated by the waterproof rubber engine compartment lining, which while intended to keep water out, also kept in a great degree of heat.

Guderian, on his way to see Hitler, flew to Grafenwöhr on 18 June 1943 to assess the problems being experienced by the 51st and 52nd Panther Battalions. He found that not only were the Panthers still suffering from technical problems, but also the crews had not really got to grips with handling their new panzers. The weight and size of the Panther made it a challenge to manoeuvre even for former Panzer IV crews. To make matters worse, half the panzertruppen lacked combat experience, which in light of them transitioning to a brand new tank type seemed a recipe for disaster.

'New equipment must be held back (that is to say, for the time being, Tigers, Panthers and heavy assault guns [Elefant]),' wrote Guderian 'until the new weapon is available in sufficient quantity to ensure a decisive surprise success. Premature commitment of new equipment simply invites the enemy to produce an effective defence against it by next year, which we shall not be able to cope with in the short time available.'

To Guderian's dismay, the new Panther units were under orders to load their tanks onto railcars ready for deployment to the Eastern Front. It would take almost a week for them to reach their disembarkation point at Borisovka. In Guderian's eyes Kursk was to prove a premature debut for the unreliable Panther.

By this stage the German Army was hoping optimistically to equip all the panzer divisions on the Eastern Front with a Panther battalion within the next six months. However, it was decided to keep the 51st and 52nd Panther Battalions together to create Panzer Regiment 39 under Meinrad von Lauchert. Fittingly, he had been with the 4th Panzer Division when it came up against the T-34 at Mzensk in October 1941.

By late June 1943 around 200 rebuilt Panthers had been issued to Panther Regiment von Lauchert and the 1st Panzer Battalion of Grossdeutschland to create the 10th Panzer Brigade. This was assigned to 4th Panzer Army's 48th Panzer Corps. On paper the Panthers of this brigade formed the single most powerful armoured unit of all the panzer forces committed at Kursk.

On unloading from the trains at Borisovka two Panthers immediately suffered engine fires and were write-offs. This was a warning of things to come. By 5 July, when Operation Citadel commenced, there were 184 operational Panthers, but within two days this had fallen to just 40.

Major General FW von Mellenthin, Chief of Staff of 48th Panzer Corps, which had over 300 panzers and 60 assault guns, noted:

> Grossdeutschland was a very strong [panzergrenadier] division with a special organization. It mustered about 180 tanks, of which 80 were part of a 'Panther Detachment' commanded by Lieutenant Colonel von Lauchert, and the remainder were in the panzer regiment.

Panzer Regiment 39 only reached Grossdeutschland's assembly area north of Moshchenoye late in the day on 4 July. This meant that it missed the division's opening attack at 0400 hours the following day. Frustratingly, at 0815 von Lauchert's Panthers lurched forward, only to lose at least four tanks to fuel leak fires. By this stage there must have been much swearing and cursing from the crews. Nonetheless, when 51st Battalion, under captain Heinrich Meyer and 52nd, under Major Gerhard Tebe, finally deployed they covered an area some 500m wide and around 3km long.

Thanks to Soviet artillery, which had set fire to the rolling cornfields, Grossdeutschland's engineers were slow in breaching the Red Army's extensive and clearly deadly defences. As a result, when the Panthers reached the 80m wide Berezovyi Ravine they were immediately held up. A number rumbled down to follow a cleared path, only to have their drives fail trying to get out the other side. Once again reliability was causing operational problems.

In total, about 25 Panthers found themselves immobilised in the ravine due to breakdowns, mines and the mud. As the tension rose, so did the stress levels of the beleaguered crews, whose sense of annoyance was escalating. Desperately the drivers tried to back up, but the Panthers did not want to reverse up the muddy banks. Engines began to overheat and drive-sprocket teeth were damaged. When some of the Panthers attempted to shift westward they promptly ran into a Soviet minefield causing yet more delay.

It was not until early afternoon that a better crossing was established 1.5km to the west and 30 Panthers, 15 Panzer Mk IVs and four battalions of infantry finally traversed Berezovyi Ravine. At Cherkasskoye the Panthers helped mop up Soviet resistance and thwarted a counter-attack. The Ausf D, lacking a ball-mounted hull machine gun (though a crude weapon port was provided) in the heat of battle had to rely on the coaxial machine gun mounted in the turret next to the main 75mm armament for defence against infantry attack.

The Panther's performance on that opening day of the Battle of Kursk had been extremely disappointing. It showed up the lack of battalion-level training, and highlighted poor communication with the chain of command. On 6 July the performance was little better and the regiment got lost.

Near Alekseyevka the Grossdeutschland ran into a T-34 tank regiment that was well dug in, thereby presenting a very low profile. Some 2km east of Cherkasskoye the Panthers blundered into Soviet mines and T-34s of the 14th Tank Regiment opened up on the Panthers' flanks at ranges of 1,000-1,200 metres. A platoon leader in 5th Company, 52nd Panther Battalion, by the name of Sergeant Gerhard Brehme, had the dubious honour of commanding one of the very first Panthers to be knocked out by a T-34. Eventually the Panther's superior firepower and gunnery enabled von Lauchert to extract his forces from the ambush. Once more, though, this episode highlighted a complete lack of experience.

By the end of 6 July Panzer Regiment 39 had lost 19 tanks, having claimed only around a dozen T-34s. All in all it was not an auspicious start to the Panther's combat career. The following day, while trying to take Dubrova, the Panthers once again presented their side armour to the enemy, this time to dug in T-34s of the 16th Tank Regiment and 85mm anti-tank guns of the 756th Anti-Tank Battalion. When they ran into a minefield east of Syrtsev some 15 Panthers were hit. Once more the Panther's L/70 gun got the better of the T-34s, but at a cost of 27 Panthers knocked out that day. The battlefield became known as the 'Panther cemetery at Dubrova.'

Guderian wanted to see at first hand how the Panther was performing and his worst fears were soon realised:

I visited both the attacking fronts during the time between 10th and 15th of July; I went first to the southern and then the northern area, and talked to the tank commanders on the spot. I there gained an insight into the course that events were taking, the lack of our men's experience in the attack and the weakness of our equipment. My fears concerning the premature commitment of the Panthers were justified.

He reported the following regarding the Panther's disappointing performance:

Due to enemy action and mechanical breakdowns, the combat strength sank rapidly during the first few days. By the evening of 10 July there were only 10 operational Panthers in the front line. 25 Panthers had been lost as total write-offs (23 were hit and burnt and two had caught fire during the approach march). 100 Panthers were in need of repair (56 were damaged by hits and mines and 44 by mechanical breakdown). 60 percent of the mechanical breakdowns could be easily repaired. Approximately 40 Panthers had already been repaired and were on the way to the front. About 25 still had not been recovered by the repair service ... On the evening of 11 July, 38 Panthers were operational, 31 were total write-offs and 131 were in need of repair. A slow increase in the combat strength is observable. The large number of losses by hits (81 Panthers up to 10 July) attests to the heavy fighting.

Guderian must have been deeply vexed at the breakdown rate, especially when the faults were only minor. Combat losses were one thing, but constant breakdowns were clearly unacceptable.

Extravagantly, von Lauchert claimed that his Panthers destroyed 263 Soviet tanks from 5–14 July at ranges of 1,500 to 3,000m. In reality Panzer Regiment 39 was ambushed three times by dug-in T-34s, often on the flanks at ranges of less than 1,200m, which casts extreme doubt on the veracity of such claims. Although Hitler had categorically instructed that no Panthers were to fall into the Red Army's hands, seven were captured on 19 July and Guderian's fears came to fruition.

Following the Soviet counter-offensive at Belgorod the 52nd Panther Battalion, with only 27 operational Panthers and 109 under repair, was obliged to blow up 72 at Tomarovka and retreat. By the time they reached Akhtyrka just nine Panthers remained operational. A subsequent report on 20 July 1943 indicated that 41 Panthers were operational, 85 repairable, 16 severely damaged and needing repair in Germany, 56 burnt out due to enemy action, and two destroyed by engine fires. By 11 August 1943 the numbers of total write-offs had risen to 156, with only nine tanks operational.

It is self-evident that the Panther's baptism of fire at Kursk, against Guderian's wishes, had been a complete and utter disaster. General von Mellenthin summed up Guderian's disappointment after Kursk saying, 'the Panthers were still in their infancy and were a failure.'

Clearly the crews needed more time to learn how to handle the Panther effectively, but Hitler did not have time. As a result the crews paid the price, as they blundered inexpertly around the battlefield. The very mistakes that had been made with Panzer Regiment 39 were to be repeated on a much bigger scale the following year during the Battle of Arracourt in France.

Perhaps inevitably, the haste with which the Panther had been designed, and the speed with which it had been put into mass production, resulted in numerous teething problems. The engine suffered cooling issues that resulted in very unwelcome engine fires. The complicated suspension and tracks also gave the crews trouble, with frequent breakages. The reality was that in the first few months of the Panther's entry into service there were far greater losses to breakdowns than to enemy action. It was not an auspicious start for Hitler's T-34 killer.

The Panther Ausf D was first deployed operationally in support of Hitler's Operation Citadel, his attack on the Soviet salient at Kursk in the summer of 1943. Engine fires, and gearbox/transmission and track failures meant many of them broke down. As a result the Red Army captured at least seven and was able to learn the Panther's secrets. This captured Panther was from the 52nd Panzer Battalion. Soviet gunnery was good, judging by the dents to the gun mantlet.

Soviet troops examine the shattered remains of a Panther: this tank has thrown its tracks and lost its turret. During the opening stages the inexperienced Panther crews kept getting stuck, lost and ambushed.

Colour Plates

The appearance of Hitler's panzers in terms of paint schemes varied enormously and the Panther was no exception. In accordance with German Army Memorandum No.181, dated 18 February 1943, the basic overall colour for all German military vehicles was a deep sand-yellow (*dunkel gelb*). From this point all vehicles were sprayed this colour, which superseded the previous panzer grey (*dunkel grau*), before leaving the factory.

This memorandum also introduced a new camouflage pattern painting system, which employed two other colours: olive green (*oliv grun*) and a chestnut or red-brown (*rotbraun*). This revolutionised the art of vehicle camouflage – but did not necessarily provide for a great deal of standardisation, as painting the camouflage was left to the local field commanders, often at platoon level. Each vehicle was supplied to its unit with tins of olive green, chestnut brown and sand yellow paint for the crew to apply.

The paints were in paste form and could be diluted with water, oil or petrol, which gave widely varying depths of colour. Paint could be applied with a spray gun, paintbrush, broom or rag. The application of textured Zimmerit anti-magnetic paste meant that the results of painted camouflage varied, as it was often hard to over paint.

Camouflaged patterns employed in the field varied from dappling effect for wooded areas to crazy paving (narrow zig-zag lines) for fighting in open country. This meant that the green and brown could be applied in spots, stripes, splinter patterns or even large lobed areas. Towards the end of 1944 some Panthers were painted in what has been dubbed the 'ambush' pattern. This consisted of large spots of olive green and chestnut brown over the sand yellow. These were then speckled with smaller spots of the other two colours. This was designed to simulate the shadows caused by sunlight filtering through foliage. Once physical camouflage employing netting with foliage was applied the vehicle became difficult to detect even at close range.

Panthers sported two-tone camouflage with green and yellow, and three-tone camouflage including the brown on the Eastern and Western fronts. Panthers captured in France were coated with Zimmerit, painted with sand yellow and over-sprayed in olive green. During the Ardennes offensive Panthers mostly sported the three-tone scheme rather than the ambush pattern. However, Jagdpanthers were seen carrying the ambush scheme. Unit identification numbers, either red edged with white or black edged with white, were normally painted on either side of the turret. The location of the German cross, black with white borders and known as the Balkan Cross or *Balkenkreuz,* varied enormously.

Panther Ausf D (front & back)
From the front the Ausf D is readily identifiable by the rectangular driver's port and the machine-gun letterbox on the glacis plate. This type and subsequent models came off the production line finished in Zimmerit anti-magnetic paste and *dunkel gelb* (dark yellow). The crews in the field then added camouflage schemes, the Balkenkreuz and unit identification symbols.

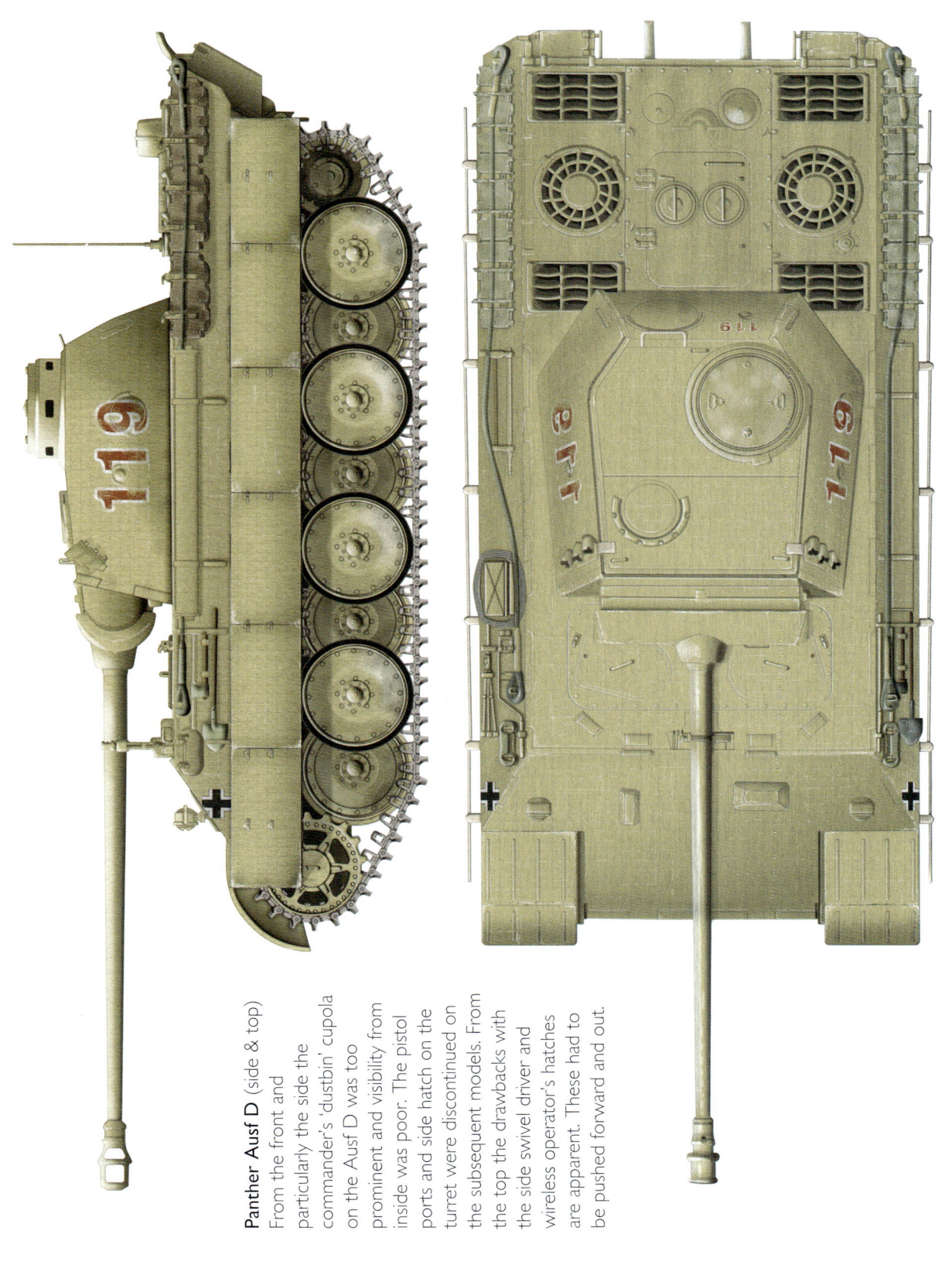

Panther Ausf D (side & top) From the front and particularly the side the commander's 'dustbin' cupola on the Ausf D was too prominent and visibility from inside was poor. The pistol ports and side hatch on the turret were discontinued on the subsequent models. From the top the drawbacks with the side swivel driver and wireless operator's hatches are apparent. These had to be pushed forward and out.

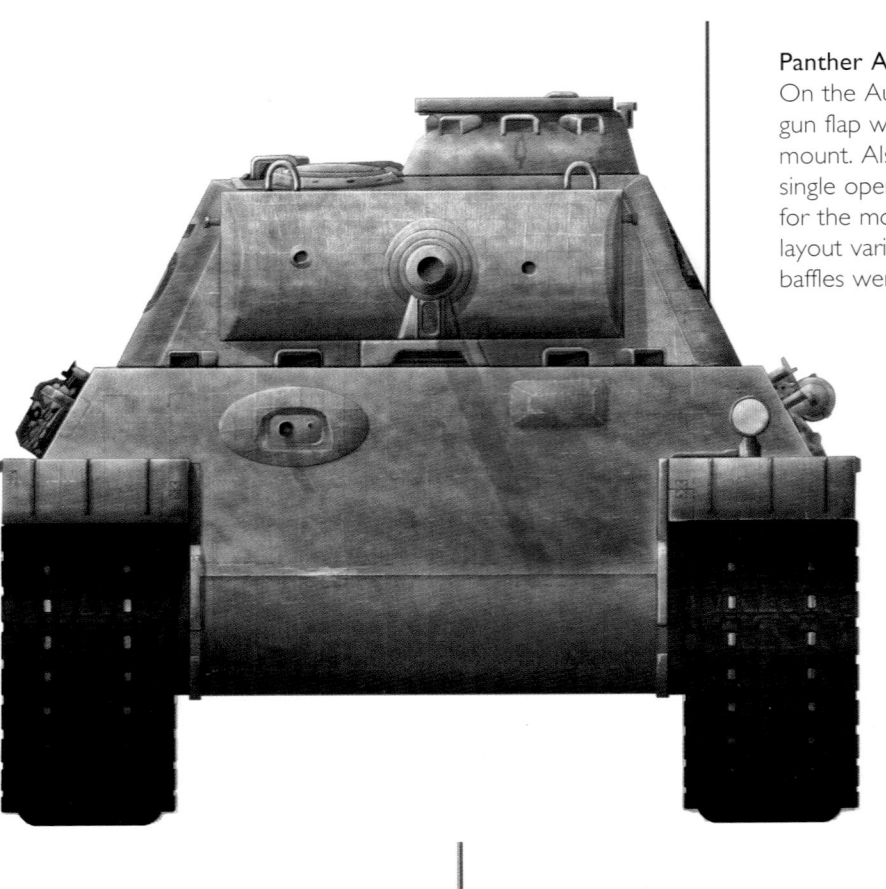

Panther Ausf A (front & back)
On the Ausf A the letterbox machine-gun flap was replaced with a proper ball mount. Also the mantlet featured only a single opening to the left of the barrel for the monocular gun sight. Exhaust layout varied on the Panther and flame baffles were fitted on the later models.

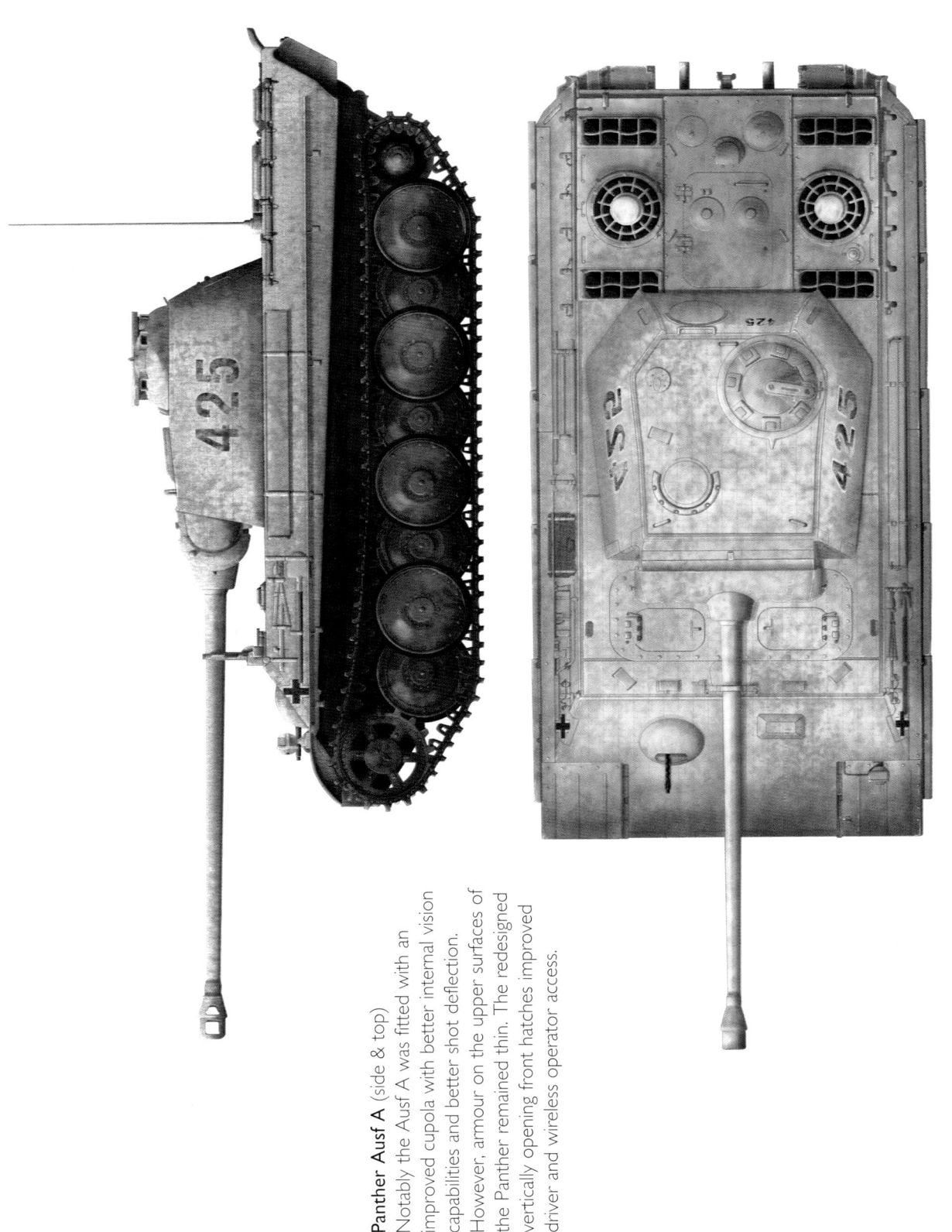

Panther Ausf A (side & top)

Notably the Ausf A was fitted with an improved cupola with better internal vision capabilities and better shot deflection. However, armour on the upper surfaces of the Panther remained thin. The redesigned vertically opening front hatches improved driver and wireless operator access.

Panther Ausf G (front & back)
On the front of the Ausf G the driver's port on the glacis plate was removed to improve armour integrity. This meant the driver had to operate either with his head out of the upper hatch, or via periscope.

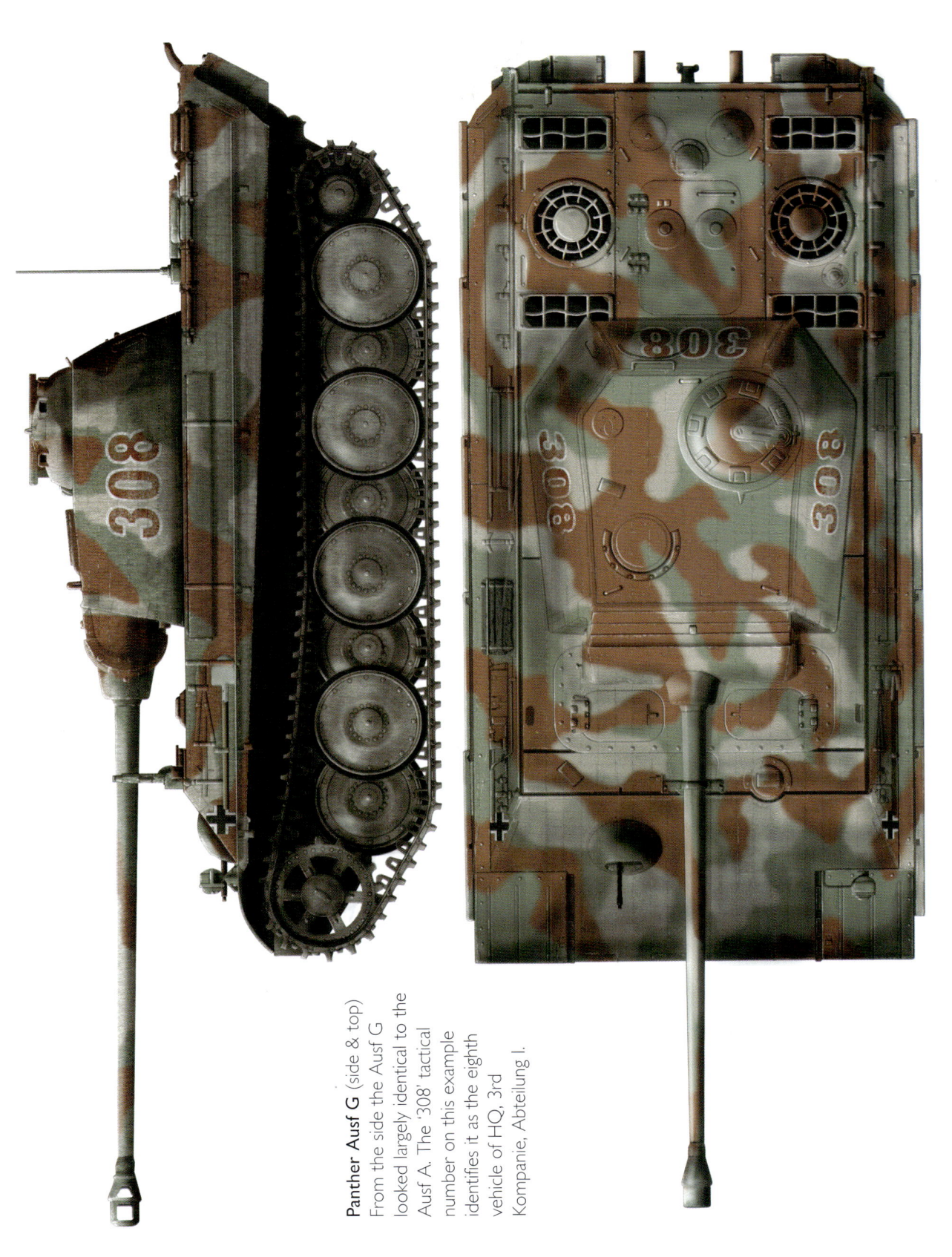

Panther Ausf G (side & top)
From the side the Ausf G looked largely identical to the Ausf A. The '308' tactical number on this example identifies it as the eighth vehicle of HQ, 3rd Kompanie, Abteilung I.

Panther Ausf F (front & back)

The Ausf F was to have featured a much narrower turret, but like the Panther II never went into production. The design wculd have been the culmination of the three earlier production variants.

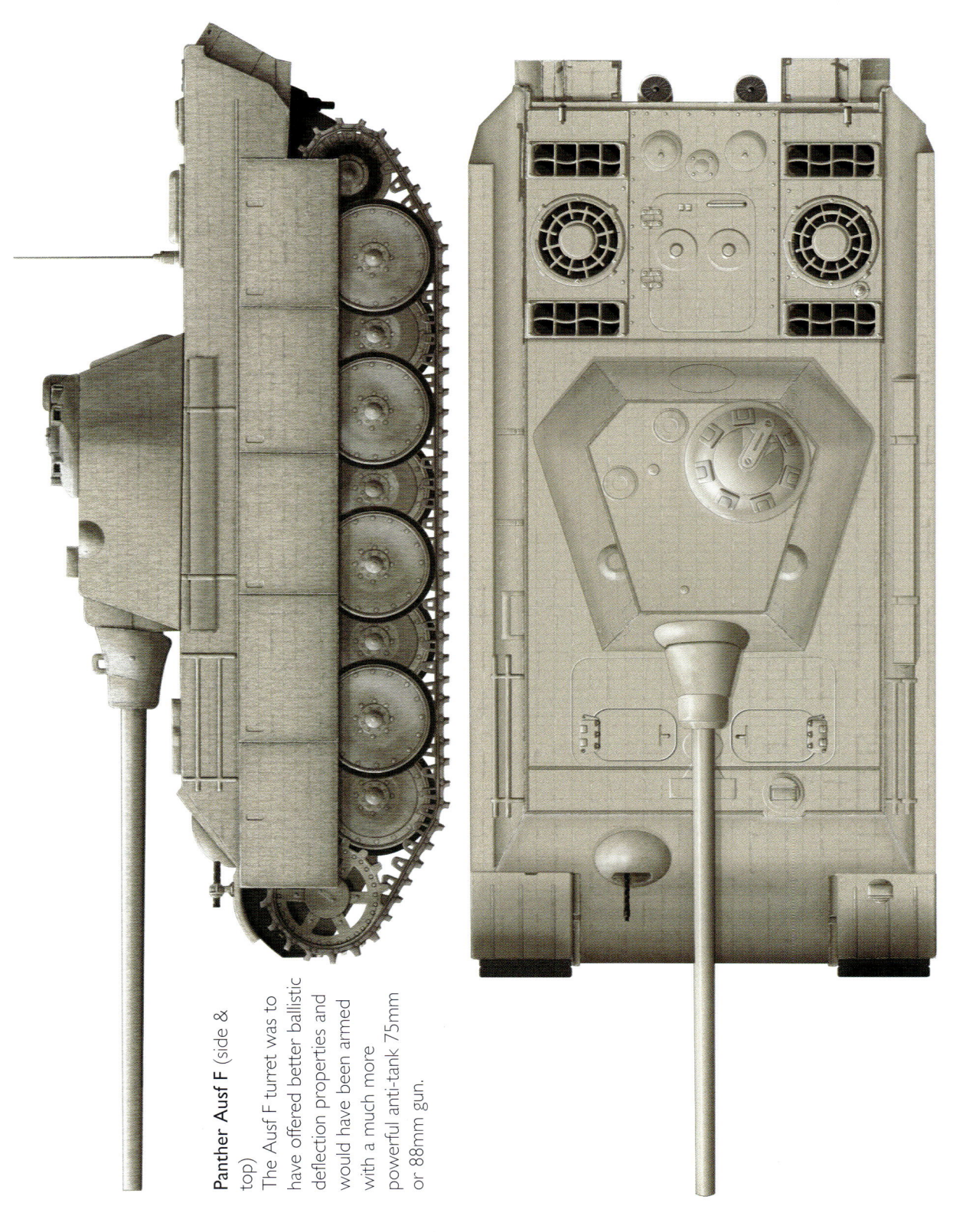

Panther Ausf F (side & top)

The Ausf F turret was to have offered better ballistic deflection properties and would have been armed with a much more powerful anti-tank 75mm or 88mm gun.

Jagdpanther (front & back)

The well-armoured Jagdpanther was a deadly killing machine that was in many ways better than the gun tank, but insufficient numbers were produced. From the front it was a similar shape to the Panther but lacked the commander's cupola. This example has the three-tone *dunkel gelb* (dark yellow), *oliv grun* (olive green) and *rotbraun* (red/brown) camouflage painted over the Zimmerit.

Jagdpanther (side & top)
The Jagdpanther offered a slightly lower profile but the gun had very limited traverse.

Bergepanther (front & back)
The weight of the Panther meant that it required a dedicated recovery vehicle, which resulted in the very crude looking Bergepanther. Photographic evidence indicates they received little more than a cursory coat of paint.

Bergepanther (side and top)
Essentially the Bergepanther comprised a turretless Panther chassis equipped with a crane and stabiliser spade. The mechanics operated from the former fighting compartment.

The front view of this Panther Ausf G preserved at the Tank Museum at Saumur, France, shows how imposing the glacis plate is. It is textured with the Zimmerit paste and has the three-tone camouflage scheme.

The three-quarter view highlights how the Panther's tracks mimicked those on the T-34 to spread the weight of the tank. The gun barrel is locked in the travelling position.

This Ausf A, also in the Saumur collection, is coated in Zimmerit, as are the side skirts.

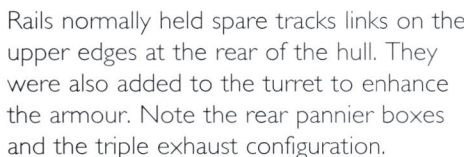

Rails normally held spare tracks links on the upper edges at the rear of the hull. They were also added to the turret to enhance the armour. Note the rear pannier boxes and the triple exhaust configuration.

The rear end of a Saumur Jagdpanther.

This damaged Ausf G commemorating the Battle of the Bulge at Houffalize, Belgium, was fished from the local river after the war.

The flattened base on the modified mantlet of an Ausf G originally preserved at Aberdeen Prov ng Ground, America, is clearly visible.

A hybrid Panther at the Tank Museum at Thun, Switzerland. It comprises an Ausf D hull with an Ausf G turret featuring the later cupola. To its left is a Jagdpanther.

Soviet KV-1 heavy tanks getting ready to launch the Red Army's counter-offensive. This armoured charge put the temperamental Panthers in headlong flight.

German mechanics working on an Ausf A's transmission. Guderian was incensed that his 'problem child' kept breaking down.

As a result of the lessons learned from Kursk the Ausf D was replaced by the Ausf A and G on the Eastern Front.

An Ausf A photographed on the Eastern Front – the muddy ground gives some idea of the conditions the panzers had to fight in. This particular Panther has lost part of its side ski·ts, known as Schürzen.

Another Ausf A with incomplete side skirts — the crew have supplemented the turret armour with spare track links.

Panzergrenadiers supporting an Ausf G — the Panther gained a tough reputation on the Eastern Front, but was never available in sufficient numbers. Nor did it replace the Panzer Mk IV as intended.

Chapter Seven

A Roman Holiday

There was no hiding Guderian's bitter disappointment over the performance of the Panther at Kursk. Reliability was to remain a bugbear throughout 1943. After the formation of the ill-fated 39th Panzer Regiment, subsequent Ausf Ds were issued to the 23rd and 26th Independent Panzer Regiments. The 1st SS, 3rd SS and 5th SS Panzer Divisions were also supplied with a limited number of Ausf D in late July 1943. The 2nd SS Panzer Division, which had been training in Germany, returned to the Eastern Front equipped with the Ausf D the following month.

The Panther did not get off to an exceptional start when it deployed to Italy. After the 1st SS Panzer Division, on occupation duties, was issued with their first batch of Panther Ausf A in September 1943, they proved so unreliable the panzertruppen rejected all of them out of hand. Once again the Panthers were sent back to the manufacturers.

The Panther did not make its presence felt in Italy again until the spring of 1944, just in time to help counter the Allies' Operation Diadem. After urgent appeals from General von Vietinghoff a company of Panther Ausf A deployed to Melfa on 15 May 1944, where they arrived five days later just in time to confront the Canadian Army.

Canadians from Vokes Force came up against the Panther in the Melfa area on 24 May 1944. The engagement resulted in the loss of four Shermans for three Panthers – it was not a good start. Nonetheless, gathering their wits, the Panther crews subsequently knocked out 17 Shermans for the loss of just five of their number as the Canadians struggled to get over the Melfa River. Clearly 21 Shermans for eight Panthers was a much better performance, and it was apparent that the crews now had a better idea of how to handle the Panther.

In the face of stiff German resistance French forces succeeded in breaching the Gustav Line on 13 May 1944 at one of its deepest points at Monte Majo. The fall of Majo unhinged the 14th Panzer Corps left wing, greatly contributing to the Allies' success. By 1730 on 23 May General B.M. Hoffmeister, commanding the Canadian 5th Armoured Division, felt a large enough breach had been achieved to commit his tanks.

It was then that the Allies first came up against the Panther in Italy. Shortly after midday the tanks of the Canadian Army's Vokes Force (British Columbia Dragoons) and supporting infantry reached their objective about two miles north-west of Aquino and Griffin Force (Strathcona's Horse and the Westminster Regiment) was ordered forward.

Lieutenant Edward J. Perkins, with the Reconnaissance Troop of Lord Strathcona's Horse racing ahead of the main body of Vokes Force, had a near miss with a Panther. His unit was equipped with turretless M3 light tanks armed only with machine guns. He spotted an enemy half-track parked by a farmhouse and recalled:

My troop opened fire, and the crew tried to escape. Five enemy soldiers were hit, two got away. Next we encountered a Panther tank, the first that we had seen in Italy. It suddenly appeared on my right front about 300 yards away. The crew commander was standing up in the turret. I fired at him with the .50 heavy machine gun and saw him slump over. With its commander hit the Panther kept going and made no attempt to retaliate. We kept going as fast as we could.

At 1500 Perkins' troop crossed the Melfa. Having secured a bridgehead he sent for the infantry of the Westminster's A Company and the Shermans of Strathcona's A Squadron. The Shermans had to clear the south bank of enemy tanks and self-propelled guns before they could help. To the south progress was slow and 30 minutes later two Panthers and a self-propelled 88mm gun appeared and began to shell Perkins' position, as well as the Strathcona tanks on the far bank. Perkins, reinforced by Major J.K. Mahoney's Westminsters, knew the enemy armour on the north bank had to be pushed away from their bridgehead and a nearby house held by enemy troops cleared. Perkins recounts:

The SP [self-propelled] 88mm on our left was still firing at A Sqdn's tanks, and Tpr J.K. Funk of my troop offered to volunteer to destroy it with a PIAT [hand held anti-tank weapon], covered by two Bren gunners of the Westminster's A Coy. He crept to within 100 yd of the SP gun and hit it with his fourth shot. The Bren gunners shot one of the SP crew and the rest were captured. The two Panther tanks withdrew to positions about 800 yd from the house, which Maj Mahoney now occupied as his Company HQ.

Vokes Force had brushed with the Panthers early on 24 May and remarkably had managed to account for three Panthers for the loss of just four Shermans. However, while A and C Squadrons of the Strathconas were trying to cross the Melfa and drive the Panthers to the far bank, they lost 17 Shermans and claimed just five panzers, not all of which were Panthers. An infantry officer spoke of the Canadian tank crews with amazement, 'I'll never forget the way the tanks would keep coming and then one would get knocked out and then another and still they'd keep coming.'

Meanwhile, the Canadians were unable to get any anti-tank weapons over to the Strathcona/Westminster bridgehead and the Germans launched three counter-attacks using Panthers. Just before dusk three Panthers almost overran the Canadian positions. The advancing panzertruppen fired high explosives, but their aim was high and they caused no casualties. PIAT anti-tank fire made the panzers lose their nerve and they wheeled away. Fortunately by 2100 some 6-pounder anti-tank guns had got over the river and during the night artillery fire kept the Panthers at bay.

The following day the Canadians counter-attacked, finally driving the Germans away from their tenuous foothold. By the end of the two-day battle for the Melfa River bridgehead the Canadians had accounted for eight Panthers, four Panzer Mk IVs and nine self-propelled guns for the loss of 21 Shermans. The hesitancy with which the Panthers had pressed home their attacks indicated a lack of experience and training – not to mention poor intelligence regarding the strength of the Canadian bridgehead.

The Canadian Army was impressed by the performance and qualitative edge of the Panther and appreciated that it could only be tackled by weight of numbers. Summing up the Melfa battles, a staff officer with the Canadian 5th Armoured wrote:

> As for the main obstacle of the German tanks… the only reason why it was possible to make headway against their qualitative superiority was by weight of numbers… General Leese [Commanding 8th Army] was prepared to lose 1,000 tanks. As he had 1,900 at his disposal, the Panther stood a fair chance of becoming an extinct species among the fauna of S. Italy.

Fortunately for the Allies in Italy the Panther (and the Tiger for that matter) was never encountered in significant numbers. In fact the two German armies fighting in the Italian campaign largely had to rely on assault guns rather than panzers to form the backbone of their armoured units. The Germans fought a defensive war in Italy so relied heavily on fixed defences rather than mobile units.

As a result of this strategy surplus Ausf D turrets known as *Pantherturm* were used to provide defensive strongpoints in Italy. They comprised a turret fitted to a fabricated steel box; this provided a fighting compartment and living space for the crew. These boxes could be entrenched, or were stabilized on a bed of logs or rocks with earth banked up around the edges. Some were also embedded in concrete. They were used in the Hitler and Gothic Lines in Italy (and were also used on the Western and Eastern Fronts). At ground level the turrets presented a low silhouette and were often well concealed, which meant the 75mm gun took a heavy toll on advancing Allied tanks.

Manned by Field Marshal Kesselring's 10th and 14th Armies, the Gothic Line was the last major obstacle between the Allies and the Alps. This proved to be probably the best of all the German defences. As it was the very last line the Germans had much longer to prepare it, with the assistance of conscripted Italian labourers. Although the Gothic Line was never finished, it still presented a formidable barrier. The positions included these Panther tank turrets set in steel and concrete. Kesselring would no doubt have preferred Panther gun tanks, but the turrets were better than nothing.

This knocked-out Panther Ausf A was also encountered in Italy.

British troops joyriding on a Panther captured in Italy. The hull is that of an Ausf D but it has the turret of the subsequent Ausf A. The Germans designated it an Ausf A (D1).

Surplus Ausf D turrets were deployed in Italy to provide anti-tank strongpoints.

There were 48 Pantherturm deployed along the Hitler and Gothic lines in Italy. Others were used on the Atlantic and West walls as well as on the Eastern Front. By March 1945 268 Panther turrets had been used for fixed defensive positions. Some might argue they would have been better used on gun tanks.

At first glance this looks to be an Ausf A that was destroyed in Italy, losing its gun barrel in the process. However, closer inspection indicates that there is a letterbox flap on the right-hand side of the glacis plate opposite the driver's flap, making the hull an Ausf D. As the turret has the later-type cupola this tank is evidently another hybrid.

A burnt-out Ausf A. Note how the side skirts have snagged and bent back from the wheels.

Panthers and a StuG III assault gun involved in the fighting around the Anzio bridgehead in Italy in 1944.

An Ausf D photographed near Monte Cassino, Italy, in the spring of 1944. The crew are busy camouflaging their vehicle in an ambush position.

An Ausf A being examined by GIs at San Giovanni, Italy, 1944. The turret and hull have been coated in a layer of Zimmerit, chunks of which have been knocked off below the cupola and the forward edges of the turret. The vehicle's tow cable is visible on the right, indicating that the crew were trying to get the tank out of what appears to be a large bomb crater.

This Ausf G was knocked out or disabled in an Italian town. The passing locals barely give the stranded monster obstructing the road a second glance.

Chapter Eight

In Calvados Country

In the summer of 1944 the main models of Panther deployed in Normandy were the Ausf A and Ausf G. Following the D-Day landings on 6 June 1944 these were very quickly in the thick of it. In total just under a dozen panzer divisions were committed to the battle for Normandy. When the invasion commenced there were 156 Panthers deployed on the Western Front, but by the end of July this had risen to 432.

In theory the 1st battalion of each panzer regiment was equipped with the Panther, but this was not always the case. The 21st Panzer Division's organisation was largely unique in Normandy; unlike the other panzer divisions (with the exception of 10th SS) it had no Panther battalion. Instead it had an assault-gun battalion and an anti-tank battalion with towed 88mm guns. The Jagdpanther, based on the Panther chassis and armed with the 8.8cm Pak43/3, were very few in number in Normandy — about a dozen at the most — so they had little bearing on the fighting.

On arriving in Normandy Sherman crews quickly learned that their short 75mm gun could not overcome the Panther's frontal armour. Their only hope was to get a shot at the Panther's turret, which might cause some damage. Otherwise they had to slip round the sides or rear of the Panther to strike the thinner armour. Such a manoeuvre often entailed the Sherman exposing its sides. The Panther could easily overcome the Sherman's frontal armour.

Two-thirds of the tanks used by British, Canadian and Polish armoured units in Normandy were Shermans, the rest being mainly British-built Cromwell and Churchill tanks. The Cromwell cruiser tank was numerically and qualitatively the most significant British tank and, along with the Sherman, formed the main strength of the British armoured divisions. However, even armed with a 75mm gun it was inferior to the late model Panzer IVs and the Panther. Similarly, the British Churchill infantry tank, although heavily armoured, could not take any gun larger than the 75mm.

The British Sherman Firefly was the only Allied tank capable of taking on the Panther and the Tiger on equal terms in Normandy. The British-built 17-pounder (76.2mm) anti-tank gun could open up 120mm of armour at 500 yards and was either towed or mounted in limited numbers of Shermans designated the Firefly VC. Due to a shortage of 17-pounders the Fireflies were only issued one per troop.

The most powerful armoured unit deployed to Normandy was the Panzer Lehr Division under General Fritz Bayerlein, which had 99 Panzer IVs, 89 Panthers, 31 Jagdpanzer IVs, 10 Sturmegschütz IIIs and eight Tigers I/IIs, giving an impressive total of 237 panzers and assault guns. Initially Panzer Lehr was stationed in the Chartres–Le Mans–Orléans area. Fate partly favoured the Allies when it was decided to ship the Panthers of the 1st Battalion Panzer Regiment 6, which was on loan from the 3rd Panzer Division, to the Eastern Front. On 5 June 1944, the day before D-Day, the first train carrying this unit reached Magdeburg in Germany, while the last was loitering in Paris. Once the Allied landings were underway the battalion was ordered to retrace its steps. As a result the Panthers did not arrive until 10 June.

The second most powerful armoured division was the 1st SS, which fielded 103 Panzer IVs, 72 Panthers and 45 StuG IIIs during the fighting in Normandy. The 9th SS Panzer Division's Panther battalion was at Mailly-le-Camp undergoing training, which was hampered by the slow rate of new tank deliveries. Its full complement of 79 tanks was not received until mid- to late June.

The 12th SS arrived in Normandy with SS-Panzer Regiment 12, under SS-Oberstrumbannführer Max Wünche, and had an authorised strength of 101 Panzer IVs and 79 Panthers. Its actual strength was close to this, with 91 combat-ready Panzer IVs and another seven in the workshop, along with 66 Panthers and two undergoing maintenance at the beginning of June. A further 13 Panthers were despatched to the division on 7 June.

The Panthers were soon in action. On 8 June 1944 the 12th SS Panthers found Carpiquet airfield deserted by the Luftwaffe and unoccupied by the advancing Canadians. They turned on the Canadian 7th Brigade, part of the Canadian 3rd Division, driving it from Bretteville l'Orgueilleuse and Putot-en-Bessin, though the Canadians in turn recaptured Putot, claiming six Panthers. At around 2200 SS-Panzergrenadier Regiment 25, supported by the Panthers, struck toward Bretteville from three directions.

The attack from the south resulted in the platoon commander's tank being immobilised in the town and surrounded. The attack from the south-west was ordered to rescue him, but the lead tank was knocked out and driven off. In the attack from the west three Panthers were hit simultaneously by concealed Canadian anti-tank guns. Two managed to withdraw, but the other burned like a torch though its crew managed to escape. The following morning the attack was broken off.

On 9 June Panthers of 3rd Company, SS-Panzer Regiment 12, under SS-Obersturmführer Rudolf von Ribbentrop, having missed the attack on Bretteville, moved on Norrey with the Caen-Cherbourg railway embankment protecting its right flank. Ribbentrop had been wounded so Hauptmann Lüdman led his 12 Panthers. However, once beyond the cover of the railway bank, well-concealed anti-tank guns knocked out seven tanks and the advance was halted. Crew losses were also heavy, with 18 of the 35 men involved killed.

At the village of Buron, north-west of Caen, elements of SS-Panzergrenadier Regiment 25 were surrounded and on the verge of being overrun by Canadian tanks. Kurt Meyer, commanding the 12th SS, was at the Ardenne monastery. He recalled the dramatically unfolding events:

> The tank kompanie of von Ribbentrop with its fifteen Panthers deployed against this mass of enemy tanks and they shot up the enemy armour halting its advance. The last enemy tank was destroyed only 100 metres west of Ardenne but von Ribbentrop had saved the command post. His initial instructions had been to relieve the panzergrenadiers and clear the Canadians from Buron, however he was distracted by the Canadian armour to the left of the village and had to send a platoon of Panthers to deal with them. Reaching Buron von Ribbentrop's Panthers knocked out several Canadian tanks.

Unwilling to enter the village without infantry support, von Ribbentrop quickly found the tables turning, as he noted:

> Just then a well-camouflaged Canadian anti-tank gun must have opened fire, because two or three tanks to my right went up in flames one after another. There was nothing left to do but pull back to our starting position and support the hard pressed infantry from there.

SS-Unterscharführer Freiberg, serving with Ribbentrop, found himself in one of the three Panthers knocked out:

> We crossed the open field to the wall around the village of Buron at high speed. As we moved past an opening in the wall, there were suddenly two explosions. Sepp Trattnick's tank and another tank burst into flames. We immediately opened fire with both machine guns on the opening of the wall. I saw some movement there and then a flash from the muzzle of an anti-tank gun. The round struck our gun mantlet and the solid projectile ended up in the fighting compartment. Our sight was smashed, and the gunner was wounded in the face. I received several fragments in my left arm.

After fighting on the Eastern front the 2nd Panzer Division made the most of its well-earned rest in France and by late May/early June 1944 Panzer Regiment 3 had 98 Panzer IVs and 79 Panthers. Frustratingly, the Panther battalion with 52 operational tanks did not arrive until 19 June; 20 were damaged in transit. For the rest of June the division fought in the Caumont area, although the Panthers were despatched to resist the British Epsom offensive.

When the British broke through east of Tilly-sur-Seulles, on the front held by Panzer Lehr, on 25 and 26 June, the 12th SS, supported by the 1st Battalion Panzer Regiment 3, counter-attacked on the right. On the 28th the Panthers destroyed 53 British tanks and 15 anti-tank guns. By 1 July they had claimed 89 enemy tanks, 13 Bren carriers and 19 anti-tank guns for the loss of 20 panzers. By early July the division still had 85 Panzer IVs in the field, with another 11 in the shop and 21 operational Panthers and 38 undergoing maintenance.

The 9th SS counter-attacked on 29 June at 0700 on the left of the Odon. Walter Harzer, Chief Operations Staff Officer of the 9th SS, observed:

As it was, our counter-offensive broke down under air attack and artillery fire, particularly the heavy guns of the battleships. They were devastating. When one of those shells dropped near a Panther, the 56-ton tank was blown over on its side, just from the blast. It was these broadsides from the warships, more than the defensive fighting of the enemy's troops, which halted our division's Panzer Regiment.

During the fighting against the Epsom salient the 9th SS lost sixteen Panzer IVs, six Panthers and 10 StuG IIIs. By the beginning of July the unrelenting operational commitment of the panzers was taking its toll; 58 per cent of the Panthers and 42 per cent of the Panzer IVs were in the maintenance depots. At this stage the 12th SS had lost 51 Panzer IVs and 32 Panthers. By the evening of 25 July the 9th SS was able to muster 18 Panzer IVs, 18 Panthers and 11 assault guns, but with their maintenance teams working full-time three days later the total stood at 22 Panzer IVs, 20 Panthers and 22 assault guns.

On 11 July Panzer Lehr counter-attacked the Americans at Le Désert and made some ground. The attack, launched in the early hours, caused the American 30th Infantry Division problems, though the initial success of the panzers was due to a gap between the American 39th and 47th Infantry Divisions south-west of Le Désert. The Americans rushed in reinforcements, but to the west a column of 10 panzers reached south of La Scellerie before losing three Panthers and being driven off.

On 18 July Montgomery threw three armoured divisions down a narrow corridor to the east of Caen and through the German defences on the Bourguébus ridge. The Panther tank played a key part in halting this armoured charge. The Panthers of the 1st SS stormed down from the ridge, forcing back the British. In the process of trying to drive them back to Caen-Troarn the 1st SS and 21st Panzer Divisions lost 109 tanks, while by the end of the first day the British had suffered 1,500 casualties and 200 tanks destroyed for the gain of just six miles (10km) beyond the Orne.

However, the north-south line from Frénouville to Emiéville held and with the commitment of the 1st SS Operation Goodwood came to a grinding halt over the next few days. The 1st SS, 12th SS and 21st Panzer effectively hemmed in the British armour. By this point west of Bourguébus at Verrières on the far side of the Caen-Falaise road the 1st SS had gathered 70 Panzer IVs and Panthers.

Just prior to Operation Cobra Panzer Lehr had 80 tanks, of which only 15 Panzer IVs and 16 Panthers were operational and rated suitable only for defensive missions. When the Americans launched Cobra on 25 July it was the Panther tanks that were at the front. Luckily Fritz Bayerlein's Panzer IVs had been withdrawn to form a reserve and in fact only a few Panthers and tank destroyers were lost to the preliminary bombing.

Panzer Lehr weathered the first bombardment on the 24th, losing just 350 men and 10 vehicles. The following day the bombing cost the division 1,000 men and numerous vehicles caught near the Periers-St Lô road; in particular a number of Panther tanks were lost. By the end of the month the Panthers had not been able to stop the Americans breaking out of the Normandy bridgehead and coherent German resistance collapsed.

Fritz Bayerlein was not a big fan of the Panther in Normandy. Highlighting its shortcomings, he noted 'While the PzKpfw IV could still be used to advantage, the PzKpfw V proved ill-adapted to the terrain. The Sherman, because of its manoeuvrability and height, was good... [the Panther was] poorly suited for hedgerow terrain because of its width. Long gun barrel and width of tank reduced manoeuvrability in village and forest fighting.' The Panther was to suffer from exactly the same problems during Hitler's Ardennes offensive.

In southern France the performance of the Panther was to be equally disappointing. During September 1944 half a dozen newly raised Panther brigades failed to secure victory for Hitler's counter-offensive against Patton's US 3rd Army at Arracourt in Lorraine. These brigades, which included Panzer Mk IVs, were poorly organised and lacked vital supporting units. Predominantly made up of armour, they operated without reconnaissance troops so had to go into battle almost blind. The crews were poorly trained and poorly led. This lack of preparedness echoed the experiences of Panzer Regiment 39 at Kursk.

These new Panther brigades were intended for the Eastern Front where they could have acted as a powerful mobile reserve. The Red Army often lacked tactical support and could not always call on adequate anti-tank weapons, artillery or close air support. In contrast in Lorraine the Panthers were thrown against American and French tanks, which were well supported by anti-tank guns, artillery and dive-bombers.

US tankers had, by this stage, developed innovative tactics against the panzers. American Shermans and supporting tank destroyers, on encountering enemy armour, would open fire with everything they had. Experienced US tank battalions, when running into Panthers, often fired phosphorous smoke rounds. The acrid smoke drawn into the Panther's ventilator could cause their crews to bail out in panic. Likewise the use of high-explosive rounds sometimes had the same result. Even if the panzertruppen stayed with their tank, the smoke obscured their gunnery sight.

The inexperienced Panther crews became the victims of a turkey shoot. They exposed their weak side armour and failed to press home their attacks when the going got tough – even though they could have easily overpowered their weaker opponents. By the time the Lorraine counter-offensive came to a halt, the Germans had lost 118 Panthers and a similar number of Panzer IVs.

The Panther often struggled in the close confines of the Normandy hedgerows or *bocage*. These Ausf G are heavily camouflaged in an effort to ward off air attack.

German infantry hitch a lift during the fighting in Normandy. The Allies encountered both the Ausf A and G in France.

A British 6-pounder anti-tank gun crew take a close look at an Ausf A. Most Panther battalions deployed to counter the allied invasion of France were equipped with the A model.

A Panther blown upside down – naval gunfire and heavy bombers proved devastating against the panzers in Normandy. This shot gives some idea of the complexity of the interleaved road wheels.

A Burning Ausf A belonging to the 2nd SS Panzer Division destroyed by the Americans at Sainteny, 8km south-west of Carentan, in July 1944.

US fighter-bomber aviators inspect their handiwork. They caught this Ausf A belonging to the Panzer Lehr Division on a narrow country road. The engine deck has been torn away, along with the tracks and rear idlers.

Another of Panzer Lehr's Ausf As destroyed at Le Désert, north of St Lô.

Yet another Ausf A belonging to Panzer Lehr, which seems to have been abandoned following an air attack.

This Ausf A belonging to the 116th Panzer Division was abandoned in Argentan in August 1944, just as the Battle for Normandy came to a close.

Three captured Ausf As in September 1944, south of Trevières in France. They are coated with Zimmerit, painted with sand-yellow and over-sprayed with olive green.

Chapter Nine

Panthers in the Bulge

Through the spring and summer of 1943 the Panther had been a disappointment. By the following summer it had proved its worth in Italy, Normandy and in Russia, even if reliability was still an issue. From March 1944 Daimler-Benz, MAN and MNH were churning out the Ausf G that finally seemed to have put to rest the earlier models' shortcomings. The only problem for the German Army was that the Panther, like the Tiger, was simply never available in sufficient numbers. In the winter of 1944 Hitler massed the greatest concentration of Panthers for his Ardennes offensive through Belgium. Army Group B had approximately 450 available; the largest concentration of Jagdpanthers was also gathered to take part in the battle for the Ardennes.

Fortunately for the Allies, the Panther's stand-off capability was nullified by the close-quarter combat in the Ardennes. As a result the Panthers fell victim to bazookas as well as 37mm, 57mm and 75mm anti-tank guns. American artillery fire was also to take its toll. Nonetheless, American Sherman crews had legitimate concerns about the superiority of enemy armour. Opposing the Panther, Panzer Mk IV, Tiger I and Tiger II was the standard American 33-ton M4 Sherman, still equipped with the short-barrelled 75mm gun. While the Sherman could fight the Mk IV on roughly equal terms, it could only kill a Panther with a shot to the rear or side armour.

The Sherman's only real advantage was a greater rate of fire thanks to gyro-stabilisation and power traverse. It also had slightly better mobility due to its lighter weight. Some Shermans were up-gunned with an improved long-barrelled 76mm high-velocity gun, but these were not available in any great quantities. The Sherman's 75mm gun, and the 76mm gun that was both towed and fitted to the self-propelled tank destroyers, were normally ineffective against the Panther's frontal armour. However, experienced American crews knew that side or rear shots would deliver a deathblow, and that a shot to the Panther's drive sprocket would immobilise it. This, however, normally involved lying in ambush and nerves of steel.

On Saturday 16 December 1944 German artillery heralded Hitler's surprise offensive and for the next five weeks his panzers fought to reach Brussels and Antwerp in what became known as the Battle of the Bulge. While the Panther helped form the backbone of the panzer forces committed to the battle, it was also given a very unusual deception role. Five days into the offensive special operations commander SS-Obersturmbannführer Otto Skorzeny, watching from a hill overlooking the battlefield, witnessed 10 Panthers from his Panzer Brigade 150, crudely disguised as American tanks, attack along the Warche Valley as part of Operation Griffon. Skorzeny had been personally appointed by Hitler to command Panzer Brigade 150, which was tasked with capturing the vital Meuse bridges at Amay, Andenne or Huy.

Skorzeny had been summoned to Hitler's Rastenburg HQ on 22 October 1944 and instructed to lead an armoured force of 3,300 men. This was to be no ordinary outfit, for they were to pass themselves off as withdrawing American troops, fully kitted out with American uniforms, weapons and vehicles. To create an effective illusion Skorzeny needed 15 Sherman tanks, 20 self-propelled guns, 20 armoured cars, 120 trucks, 100 jeeps and 40 motorcycles. Despite the vast numbers of American military vehicles captured by the Germans in the preceding months, Skorzeny found the hard-pressed frontline commands reluctant to give up their precious booty.

Under Operation Rabenhügel, Oberkommando West divided the requisition of equipment for Skorzeny's mission between the three Army Groups in the West. Army Group G was ordered to provide eight American tanks and 20 trucks; Army Group H was to provide two tanks and 50 jeeps and Army Group B five tanks and 30 jeeps, which were to be delivered to Skorzeny's training area at Grafenwöhr.

In the event only 74 trucks and 57 cars arrived, along with just two broken-down Shermans and two American armoured cars. Skorzeny discovered he was the recipient of much worn-out rubbish, as 30 per cent of the vehicles needed repairs and both the Shermans were inoperable. Initially his unit was equipped with five Panthers, five Sturmgeschütz assault guns, six German armoured cars and six armoured personnel carriers. When they finally went into battle they only deployed 10 Panthers and five StuGs. There was simply no way to make a Panther look like a Sherman, so Skorzeny's men ingeniously opted to make them look like the Sherman's tank destroyer cousin, the M10 Wolverine, based on a Sherman chassis but with a much more angular hull and turret. To do this the Panthers were disguised with sheet metal, painted olive green and given prominent white five-pointed American recognition stars.

In addition, Kampfgruppe Peiper, drawn from 1st SS Panzer Division, consisted of 72 Panzer Mk IV and Panthers, about 40 King Tigers and 25 assault guns. 1st and 2nd Companies of SS-Panzer Regiment 1, forming part of Kampfgruppe Peiper, fielded 37 Panthers, mostly Ausf Gs, at the beginning of the offensive. It was almost 0400 on 17 December when the Kampfgruppe advance guard, comprising two

Panthers and three half-tracks, began the advance on Honsfeld, their initial objective. These were followed by four Mk IV flak panzers armed with 37mm cannon and two other flak vehicles with 20mm quads. The two leading Panthers entered Honsfeld and shot up the equipment of an American unit stationed there. It was not until they emerged on the other side that American anti-tank guns engaged them.

Panzer Brigade 150's three battlegroups, or Kampfgruppen, were assigned to the 1st SS and 12th SS Panzer Divisions and the 12th Volksgrenadier Division. The 1st SS and 12th SS launched the 6th SS Panzer Army's main thrusts. Skorzeny cynically noted that his fake M10s were sufficient to: 'deceive very young American troops seeing them at night from very far away.' One, coded B4, under the command of Leutnant Peter Mandt, led the attack in the direction of Malmédy and hit a mine in front of the railway overpass to the south-west of the town. B5 was disabled at Malmédy by a US bazooka team, while another, B10, crashed into the café at La Falize. B7, commanded by Oberfeldwebel Bachmann, was the only Panther to get as far as the northern bank of the Amblève River. It was brought to a halt by US bazooka fire 50m from the Warche bridge at Malmédy.

Fritz Bayerlein's Panzer Lehr Division was short of tanks, and on the night of 15 December he could only muster 57 Panthers and Mk IVs. To bolster these he received an assault gun brigade and two battalions of self-propelled tank destroyers. He cobbled together an advance guard, led by a company of Panthers, that would exploit any gains made by the 26th Volksgrenadier Division.

Crossing the Our River posed a problem because of the weight of the Panthers. The proposed bridging sites were in a deep river gorge that meant heavy equipment could not be brought up to help the German engineers. As a result all the bridging equipment had to be manhandled into place, which was a slow process. Even when a bridge was completed at Dasburg the approaching panzers found it hard to negotiate the very narrow hairpin turns. Just 10 tanks had got over before a tank took the final turn too short, crashed into the bridge and fell into the river. While the crew escaped, the unfortunate driver drowned. It took two hours to repair the damage.

On the morning of 18 December 2nd Panzer's reconnaissance battalion probed the positions of Task Force Rose at Antoniushof, and in the early afternoon the Panthers and Mk IVs, supported by Panzergrenadiers, attacked. The American infantry and artillery were put to flight, but the Shermans stayed to fight. Seven Shermans were knocked out, and when Captain Lawrence Rose and the survivors attempted to escape they ran into the 116th Panzer Division near Houffalize, 10 miles north of Bastogne. Panthers and Mk IVs equipped with new infra-red night-fighting devices overwhelmed Task Force Harper at Fe'itsch.

In the early hours of the 20th eight Panthers led the attack toward Dom

Bütgenbach. They were greeted by American artillery. The company commander's Panther was hit and caught fire and three more succumbed to the barrage. When several Panthers broke into the American positions they were illuminated by flares and a 57mm anti-tank gun crew poured four rounds into a Panther, causing it to burn; a second Panther received the same treatment. Only a blockage on the 57mm prevented the gunners from engaging a third tank, which withdrew after losing its commander.

The day before Christmas, at 2200, Panthers and Panzer IVs led by a captured Sherman from 2nd SS Panzer ran into American tanks on the road to Manhay. The Americans hesitated because elements of the US 3rd and 7th Armored Divisions were holding the line from Trois Points-Manhay-Hotton, so there were concerns about friendly fire. Panzergrenadiers armed with Panzerfausts swiftly destroyed four Shermans and severely damaged two others. Two Panthers received direct hits, but the rest of the column sped through the broken American positions.

At this point panzer ace SS-Oberscharführer (Technical Sergeant) Ernst Barkmann, commanding Panther 401, got lost and drove alone onto Highway N15. The highly decorated Barkmann was a veteran of the Eastern Front and Normandy, who along with his unit, SS-Panzer Regiment 2, had re-equipped with the Panther in early 1944. The experiences of Barkmann and his crew in the Ardennes were typical of the confused and chaotic nature of the fighting there. While experience was invaluable, luck also played its part.

In the darkness Barkmann, assuming his comrades were in front of him, pressed on. Some 50 metres ahead and to the right he saw a tank with its commander standing in the turret. Assuming it was from the 2nd SS Barkmann drew up to the left-hand side of the tank. Instructing his driver to kill the engine, he removed his radio headset. At that point the other commander dropped into his tank and slammed the hatch shut. Then the driver's hatch popped open on the other tank and Barkmann noticed the instrument panel light was not the same as a Panther's (wine red rather than green).

Realising it was an American-crewed Sherman, he ordered his gunner to fire. The gunner traversed, only to catch the L/70 gun barrel on the enemy's turret. The impact jammed the Panther's turret. The quick-thinking driver started the engine and backed up a few yards, and the gunner slammed a round into the rear of the Sherman. Rumbling past the burning enemy tank, Barkmann spotted two more Shermans coming from the forest on the right of the road. These were also dealt with in quick succession. Then, rounding a large S-bend, Barkmann ran into nine partially dug-in American tanks. He ordered his driver to press through them and for some reason the enemy tanks did not engage. Instead the American crews bailed out.

Barkmann's Panther reached Manhay, only to be confronted by three Shermans coming from the direction Barkmann needed to take toward Grandmenil and Érezée. Heading north-west he rumbled past yet more enemy tanks that were parked with their crews dismounted. The Americans watched as the Panther roared by, then, waking to the danger, leapt into their tanks, but as they were nose to tail they could not target Barkmann. The Panther's crew hastily threw out a smoke bomb to cover their escape. Barkmann estimated they passed more than 80 enemy tanks, having stumbled into the assembly area for the US 7th Armored Division, as well as the US 82nd Airborne and 75th Infantry Divisions.

The chaos did not there. An American jeep ran headlong into the Panther, which crushed it, but in doing so crashed into a stationary Sherman. The Panther's drive sprocket became entangled in the Sherman's tracks and its engine stalled. The driver restarted the engine and backed up, successfully freeing the Panther. It rolled on past more American vehicles and equipment, but now with Shermans in pursuit.

Barkmann coolly traversed his turret and knocked out the lead tank. Repeating the action several times, he succeeded in closing off the road behind him. He and his men finally took shelter in the forest and calmly dismounted to take the morning air and marvel at their luck. At such close quarters Panther 401 could have been destroyed numerous times. As they stood about they could hear Panthers firing from the direction of Manhay. Retracing his steps to rejoin their company, Barkmann counted 20 American tanks that had surrendered.

After Christmas Hitler's Ardennes offensive very quickly lost momentum, especially once the weather cleared and Allied fighter-bombers set about the panzers. In addition a shortage of fuel proved to be the panzers' greatest weakness. After the withdrawal of Kampfgruppe Peiper at least 15 Panthers were left in La Gleize and Stoumont. One of those abandoned in La Gleize was a rare Ausf G produced as a trial vehicle for the new suspension, with the steel-rimmed 'silent-block' wheels that were to be standardised on the proposed Ausf F.

By mid-January 1945, 282 Panthers had reportedly survived the Battle of the Bulge, of which just 97 were listed as operational. When the Allies crossed the Rhine later in 1945 very few Panthers remained in the West. Most had already been sent east to take part in Hitler's doomed counter-offensive against the Red Army in Hungary.

A bloodied and dazed panzertruppe staggers away from his burning Panther Ausf G on 17 December 1944. Hitler massed over 400 Panthers for his Ardennes offensive, but many of them were non-operational.

Panther 413, an Ausf G belonging to SS-Panzer Regiment 1, is clearly a combat casualty, but during the fighting in the Ardennes operational availability and mechanical attrition rates still beset the Panther fleet. It would have taken a massive blast to flip this 45-ton tank.

American officers pose by the rear of a snow-covered Panther Ausf G. The rear turret access hatch is open, indicating that it may have been abandoned. Likewise the rear pannier is open, suggesting the crew were rummaging for tools. Fuel was in such short supply that when it ran out many panzertruppen were obliged to leave their vehicles at the roadside. In the case of this particular tank, the far side idler is missing, as are the tracks. It has been fitted with flame-trap exhaust mufflers.

Another Panther lost during the winter of 1944–45. The Panzer IV in the foreground has rear-ended it. However, it is likely both tanks were shunted off the road after being knocked out.

American GIs take a closer look at one of Panzer Brigade 150's Panthers disguised as an M10 tank destroyer –the double baffle muzzle brake meant it looked more like the American M36.

Close-up of the plating added to the turret. The Panthers modified to masquerade as M10s were painted Olive Drab, with thickly ringed white stars on the additional armour added to the glacis and turret sides.

Another Panther disguised as an M10, coded B10, crashed into a café at La Falise while backing up. This shot gives a good idea of the lengths taken to make the turret look like an American tank destroyer.

B7 was the only Panther/M10 tc reach the northern bank of the Amblève at Malmédy. It was 50m from the bridge when a bazooka round in the engine compartment brought it to an abrupt halt. All but one of the crew were killed trying to get back over the bridge by foot. Interestingly, this particular tank has no muzzle brake – it is possible it was removed as part of the deception exercise.

The Jagdpanthers were too few in number to make much impact in the Battle of the Bulge. This one, being given the once over by a GI, has the bolted-on mantlet collar.

An American M36 tank destroyer takes a closer look at a knocked-out Jagdpanther.

An immobilised Panther stranded in a sea of mud. By mid-January just 97 remained operational.

An overturned and partially submerged Panther at Houffalize in Belgium. The bridge was rebuilt after the tank went into the water. Note the hole ripped in the baseplate armour. By 25 December 1944 the Panzers had got as far as Celles, just east of Dinat on the Meuse, but by 16 January 1945 they had been driven back to Houffalize.

Burnt-out Panthers caught in the open in the Ardennes. At least 15 Panthers were abandoned at La Gleize and Stoumont during the Battle of the Bulge.

A Panther Ausf G, with the anti-ricochet gun mantlet, and a Panzer Mk IV destroyed in the fighting for Hotton north-west of Bastogne.

Panther Ausf A (DI) '322' on the Eastern Front in the winter of 1944–45. It sports a whitewash paint job and the turret and hull have been finished with Zimmerit.

Chapter Ten

Panther or T-34?

For a long time the Panther was described as the best tank of the Second World War. Certainly it was a vast improvement on the Tiger I, which although an excellent tank killer was costly, time-consuming to build and ultimately unwieldy on the battlefield. Most notably, the Panther's 75mm gun was much better than the one installed in the Panzer Mk IV. Likewise the Panther's gun had better penetrating power than the Tiger's 88mm KwK 36 L/56 gun because of its faster muzzle velocity.

While the Panther had a huge advantage thanks to its excellent main armament, in comparison to the T-34 in terms of reliability, armoured protection and mobility it was nonetheless found wanting. It was the T-34 that helped Stalin seize the operational initiative in Ukraine and Byelorussia, whereas the Panther singularly failed Hitler. Mikhail Koshkin ensured that the Red Army had a tank that by 1943 was easy to produce, had superior mobility and crucially was reliable in all conditions.

In contrast, the heavy Tiger and medium Panther had to move up to their operational areas by train or face continual mechanical breakdowns. Trains were always vulnerable to air attack and sabotage. Since 1941 Guderian had wanted a panzer with superior mobility to the T-34, but he never got it. MAN's engineers designed the chassis and running gear for a 24-ton tank, which ended up at 45 tons with predictable results. The severely strained engine and transmission kept failing. The Panther units at Kursk were beset by what were called 'teething problems', but in reality these shortcomings afflicted the Panther for much of its operational life.

The 75mm KwK40 L/43 gun on the Panzer Mk IV F2 could penetrate up to 82mm of armour at 1,000m, easily killing a T-34 with 65mm of frontal armour. The Panther's 75mm Kwk 42 L/70 anti-tank gun was an even more formidable weapon and, firing standard armoured piercing ammunition, could penetrate 111mm of armour at 1,000m, i.e. far thicker armour than was found on any Soviet tank. The improved tungsten-core Panzergranate 40/42 round could penetrate 150mm of armour at 1,000m. This meant that the Panther was easily capable of killing a T-34 at 800m, while from the side it could manage this at three times the range.

Well-trained and experienced crews were capable of knocking out tanks at even greater ranges, though commanders usually forbade them from engaging at long ranges to avoid wasting ammunition. Both the L/70 and L/56 could penetrate targets out to 2,000m, but at such distances accuracy became a problem.

While the L/70 ensured the Panther could kill enemy tanks at far greater distances than the T-34, this advantage came at a price that was reflected in the Panther's overall performance. The larger L/70, compared to the L/43, meant a bigger turret, which needed a wider hull that was heavier and reduced mobility, thereby straining the drive train.

This stand-off capability meant that it was fatal for Soviet tanks to engage the Tiger and the Panther in the open. The T-34's 76.2mm gun could penetrate the Panther's side armour out to 1,000m, but could only penetrate the glacis armour at 300m and could not overcome the turret frontal armour. An improved Soviet armour-piercing round was not introduced until October 1943, but then it could only damage the Panther's frontal armour at ranges under 100m. Although the Panther's frontal armour was on a par with the Tiger's, it side armour was little better than the Panzer IV.

The T-34's TMFD gunner's sight was inferior to the Panther's TFZ12 sight, with a narrower field of view and poorer magnification. However, the T-34 had quicker reaction times thanks to its turret traverse. The T-34/76 could rotate at 30 degrees per second, giving it a full rotation in 12 seconds. This was five times faster than the Panther Ausf D and 50 per cent faster than the Ausf A. Once the T-34 had closed on the Panther its gunner could redirect fire much faster. Likewise the turret on the M4 Sherman could be fully rotated in 15 seconds, giving it the same advantage over the Panther in close-quarter fighting. For both the T-34 and the Sherman it was imperative they closed with the Panther as quickly as possible.

Soviet gunners tended to be trigger-happy and often with good reason. The net result was that they often fired half their ammunition in a single combat, whereas their German counterparts had to be more conservative as they could not guarantee timely reloads. The T-34/76 Model 1943 typically carried 75 High Explosive-Fragmentation and 25 Armoured Piercing-High Explosive rounds (this included four tungsten-core rounds after October 1943). The Panther normally carried an even mix of AP and HE.

In armoured warfare mobility is as important as firepower. German panzer designers at Daimler-Benz and MAN, because of their ongoing rivalry, chose to ignore the T-34's fundamental design attributes. Whereas the T-34 was a 30-ton tank with a less flammable diesel engine and rear-wheel drive, the Panther weighed in at 45 tons with a highly flammable petrol engine and vulnerable front-wheel drive. In the Ausf D the two fuel pumps were prone to leaks that caused serious engine fires. The T-34's uncomplicated Christie suspension was also ignored in favour of the complex interleaved road-wheel running gear that was easily fouled on the Eastern Front.

Although the Panther had lower ground pressure and a better road speed, especially once the T-34/85 appeared with the much heavier turret, the Panther could only move faster once it was in seventh gear – a difficult task in combat conditions. In third gear the T-34 could rumble along at 29kph (18mph), while the Panther could only manage 13kph (8mph). Added to this the Ausf D and A required almost four times as much fuel as a T-34 to cover 1km. Such poor fuel efficiency was clearly a major problem, as Germany began to feel the squeeze on its oil supplies and the Allies enjoyed ever-growing air superiority. Such shortages proved fatal in the Ardennes.

Heinz Guderian, as Inspector General of Hitler's panzer forces, knew that the Panther and Tiger were too little too late and were simply not good enough. After the war he said:

> Thus the T-34 tank was superior to the German tanks in tracks, in motors, in armour and in gun, but inferior in optics and radio and it had no turret [cupola] for the tank commander with all-round sight. When – in 1943 – the German Panther and Tiger tanks appeared on the battlefields, the superiority passed again to the Germans, but it applied only to a single tank, and not to the quantity. The Russians produced their T-34 tanks without modifications in great series, while Hitler could not be prevented from perpetually changing the types, thus causing repeated reductions of the series.

On balance Guderian acknowledged that the T-34 was the better tank.

The appearance of the T-34 in the summer of 1941 came as a shock to the panzers as it carried a larger calibre gun. Initially its performance was disappointing, but once the panzers began to suffer in the freezing Russian winter the T-34 came into its own. While the T-34 overcame its early teething problems, the Panther did not.

Panzergrenadiers gather in front of an Ausf A on the Eastern Front. Ultimately the T-34 erjoyed a better overall performance and was produced in far greater numbers.

The M4 Sherman medium tank, which formed the backbone of the American and British armies, had many shortcomings, but it also had its advantages; not least its lighter weight and reliability. Again, like the T-34, the Sherman was produced in far greater quantities than the Panther.

Besides limited tank destroyers, few tanks, such as the Sherman Firefly, offered any parity against the Panther. The Firefly was armed with a powerful 17-pounder, but the tank was still under-armoured.

While the Soviets were able to upgrade the T-34 to create the T-34/85 armed with an 85mm gun, plans for further models of the Panther never came to fruition.

A late-model Panther with the exhaust mufflers. Like the Tiger, the Panther's bulk made it particularly ill-suited for urban warfare.

An Ausf A belonging to 9th Panzer, knocked out in Cologne in early March 1945. A round has gone through the side armour into the fighting compartment, and the muzzle brake is missing.

Two views of the Panther's distinctive rear turret access hatch. This was typically used for reloading ammunition for the 75mm gun. It was also an escape route for the crew to bail out if the tank was hit.

Chapter Eleven

The Panther's Fate

Throughout the rest of the war, Germany continued to keep the great majority of Panther forces on the Eastern Front, where the situation progressively worsened in the face of the Red Army's massive gains. The highest number of operational Panthers on the Eastern Front was achieved in September 1944, when some 522 were listed as operational out of a total of 728. It was simply not enough. In January 1945, just before the end of the war, Guderian's Panzer Commission reported that on the Eastern Front the final drives of 370 Panthers had failed. As a result the panzertruppen were losing confidence in their tanks. The last recorded status report, on 15 March 1945, listed 740 Panthers on the Eastern Front with just 361 operational.

From late 1944 Hitler had intended to introduce a rationalization programme known as the Richtwert-Programm IV, which would have terminated production of all the earlier types of panzers in favour of the new generation of Panthers. These were to be supported by a family of waffenträgers and self-propelled vehicles developed from the hugely successful Czech 38(t) light tank chassis.

If the Second World War had dragged on, and had Hitler been able to maintain his planned production rates, the Panther, Panther II and Jagdpanther, and to a lesser degree the Tiger II and Jagdtiger, could have created a powerful backbone for his panzer divisions. Instead Germany's surrender in May 1945 brought to an end Hitler's remarkable panzer story and designs for the Panther's successors remained unrealized.

Post-war assessments confirmed that Allied bombing during 1944 had greatly disrupted Panther production, particularly the Maybach engine plant. Inevitably the bombing also impacted on the availability of spare parts. This in turn affected attrition rates. In addition it was found that the use of slave labour in the factories resulted in poor quality control, if not out-right sabotage. The Panther, despite all its production problems, proved to be third most produced (5,976) armoured fighting vehicle after the StuG III assault gun (9,409) and Panzer Mk IV (8,544). The Tiger I (1,354) and Tiger II (489) lagged way behind.

The victors each took a few Panther tanks home for trials. A captured Ausf A was used for anti-tank gunnery trials at Longcross range in Surrey, England. For the purpose of conducting comparative tests with the post-war British Centurion tank (which proved to be one of the best British tanks ever built), Britain constructed at least one Panther in 1946 from spare and cannibalised parts, to create a 'new' Panther. After the war numbers of Panthers served on in an operational capacity, particularly with the Bulgarian, French and Romanian armies.

Charles de Gaulle's Free French Forces obtained a considerable number of captured Panthers following the German collapse in Normandy. The French Army used some of these from 1944 to 1947, making it the operator with the longest experience of the Panther. Enough intact and repairable Panthers were gathered in France to allow the French to equip almost two battalions. They were deployed by the 501st and 503rd Tank Regiments. A captured Panther sporting the Free French Army badge was put on display in Paris in the late 1950s.

The Red Army also made some use of captured Panthers by recycling them and supplying them to their new-found allies in eastern Europe. Bulgaria received 15 Panthers of various makes (D, A and G) during March–April 1945 from captured and overhauled Soviet stocks; they only saw limited service as spares became a problem. Romania received 13 Panther tanks from the Soviets in May 1946. They were initially issued to the Romanian 1st Armoured Brigade, but in 1947 the equipment was handed over to the Soviet-organized Tudor Vladimirescu Division, which was an infantry unit converted into an armoured division. The Romanians designated the Panther the T-5.

According to British analysis, the two main reasons for the defeat of the Panther during the Second World War were being abandoned and destroyed by the panzertruppen themselves. In other words they broke down, ran out of fuel or were damaged and could not be recovered. These two categories accounted for nearly half the Panthers left on the Normandy battlefield during August 1944 and constituted 80 per cent of all the Panthers lost.

A post-war French assessment showed that the average engine lifespan of the Ausf A deployed in Normandy was 1000km (620 miles). Although the Panther engine was compact, the engine compartment was poorly ventilated and overheated. Porous fuel lines leaked petrol and fumes increased the risk of fire. Fortunately a firewall prevented engine fires from spreading into the fighting compartment. The Panther, being front heavy, quickly wore out the final drive.

While the Panther's interleaved road-wheel design may have improved stability and flotation, and enhanced the weak side armour, the wheels were too complex and time-consuming to change, especially the inner wheels. No other nation adopted this practice. Like the Tiger, the Panther's interleaved wheels had a habit of clogging when driving through compacted mud, rubble and the vegetation in the high banks of the Normandy hedgerows. On the Eastern Front the wheels could freeze solid overnight if the mud was not removed.

Air power only accounted for about 6 per cent of all the lost Panthers investigated in Normandy. Rockets and free-fall bombs were inaccurate when trying to hit vehicles and the Germans were masters of camouflage. The Allied air forces' real contribution was the sense of panic their attacks caused, with vehicle crews quickly taking to the fields at the onset of an air strike.

The Panther was a good gun tank, but it was far from perfect. Like the Tiger it was a good breakthrough weapon that could pick off enemy tanks in open country at considerable range. Where it did not excel was in the close-quarter battles, especially in the confines of Normandy and the Ardennes. Ultimately, the Panther's so-called 'teething problems' were never fully resolved. In 1943 the Panther could manage an operational reliability rate of just 35 per cent. In contrast, the rugged T-34 could manage 70–90 per cent. In the face of such attrition rates, the outnumbered Panthers were inevitably overwhelmed. Ultimately that proved to be the fate of Hitler's T-34 killer.

This Ausf G was probably one of the last to come off the production lines. It lacks the distinctive Zimmerit paste, which was applied in the factories from early 1943 until late 1944. In order to speed up delivery Zimmerit was rarely seen on vehicles produced in 1945. This Panther's hull, turret and gun barrel have a sprayed-on camouflage scheme.

A Panther Ausf A being driven by the Red Army in the Warsaw area in September 1944. The Soviets captured large numbers of Panthers, but while Soviet tank crews appreciated the superior optics and gunnery they struggled to keep them serviceable. At the end of the war the Red Army gave most of them away.

This appears to be a Panther turret strongpoint used on the Eastern Front – otherwise a Panther has been decapitated. The later-type cupola has been blown off and is lying on the ground to the left.

This looks like the same turret, photographed from a different angle. An enemy round has torn through the upper part of the gun mantlet.

British or Canadian tankers pose with their new tank. Like the Red Army, the Western Allies could only reuse Panthers for a limited time.

This Ausf G was captured by the Canadian Army in Germany in February 1945.

A family posing with a 'French Panther'. The French captured enough Panthers to equip almost two battalions, which remained in service until 1947. This one has the Free French Army badge on the turret and was displayed in Paris in the late 1950s.

This Ausf D and Tiger I, along with other Panthers, were photographed at a tank graveyard at Tomarovka. The retreating Germans destroyed about 70 immobilised Panthers on 5 August 1943.

Scrapped Panthers and a Panzer IV. This armoured vehicle graveyard was near Isigny-sur Mer in Normandy and the equipment probably came from Panzer Lehr, 2nd Panzer and 2nd SS Panzer.

The Panther retrieved from the river at Houffalize in 1947 preserved as a war memorial.

Further Reading

Forczyk, Robert, *Panther vs T-34 Ukraine 1943*, (Osprey Publishing Ltd 2007)

Forty, Jonathan, *PzKpfw V Ausf A, D & G Panzer V Panther*, (Ian Allan Publishing Ltd 2003)

Gander, J. Terry, *JgdPz IV, V, VI and Hetzer Jagdpanzer*, (Ian Allan Publishing 2004)

Guderian, General Heinz, *Panzer Leader*, (Futura Publications 1982)

Liddell Hart, B.H, *The Other Side of the Hill*, (Pan Books Ltd 1983)

Manstein, Field Marshal Erich von, *Lost Victories*, (Greenhill Books 1987)

Mellenthin, Major-General, F.W. von, *Panzer Battles*, (Futura Publications 1984)

Quarrie, Bruce, *Hitler's Teutonic Knights SS Panzers in Action*, (Patrick Stephens Ltd 1986)

Quarrie, Bruce, *Weapons of the Waffen-SS From small arms to tanks*, (Patrick Stephens Ltd 1988)

Tucker-Jones, Anthony, *T-34 The Red Army's Legendary Medium Tank*, (Pen & Sword Military 2015)

Tucker-Jones, Anthony, *Armoured Warfare in the Battle for Normandy*, (Pen & Sword Military 2012)

Tucker-Jones, Anthony, *Falaise the Flawed Victory*, (Pen & Sword Military 2008)

Williamson, Gordon, *Waffen-SS Handbook 1933–1945*, (Sutton Publishing Ltd 2003)